AI for Sports

AI FOR EVERYTHING

Artificial intelligence (AI) is all around us. From driverless cars to game winning computers to fraud protection, AI is already involved in many aspects of life, and its impact will only continue to grow. Many of the world's most valuable companies are investing heavily in AI research and development, and not a day goes by without news of cutting-edge breakthroughs in AI and robotics.

The *AI for Everything* series will explore the role of AI in contemporary life, from cars and aircraft to medicine, education, fashion and beyond. Concise and accessible, each book is written by an expert in the field and will bring the study and reality of AI to a broad readership, including interested professionals, students, researchers and lay readers.

AI for Immunology
Louis J. Catania

AI for Cars
Josep Aulinas & Hanky Sjafrie

AI for Digital Warfare
Niklas Hageback & Daniel Hedblom

AI for Art
Niklas Hageback & Daniel Hedblom

Ai for Creativity
Niklas Hageback

AI for Death and Dying
Maggi Savin-Baden

AI for Radiology
Oge Marques

AI for Games
Ian Millington

AI for School Teachers
Rose Luckin, Karine George & Mutlu Cukurova

AI for Learners
Carmel Kent & Benedict du Boulay

AI for Social Justice
Alan Dix and Clara Crivellaro

For more information about this series please visit:
https://www.routledge.com/AI-for-Everything/book-series/AIFE

AI for Sports

Chris Brady

Karl Tuyls

Shayegan Omidshafiei

CRC Press
Taylor & Francis Group
Boca Raton London New York

CRC Press is an imprint of the
Taylor & Francis Group, an **informa** business

First Edition published 2022
by CRC Press
6000 Broken Sound Parkway NW, Suite 300, Boca Raton, FL 33487-2742

and by CRC Press
2 Park Square, Milton Park, Abingdon, Oxon, OX14 4RN

CRC Press is an imprint of Taylor & Francis Group, LLC

Library of Congress Cataloging-in-Publication Data

Names: Brady, Christopher, 1947- author. | Tuyls, Karl, author. | Omidshafiei, Shayegan, author.
Title: AI for sports / Chris Brady, Karl Tuyls, Shayegan Omidshafiei.
Other titles: Artificial intelligence for sports
Description: Boca Raton, FL : CRC Press, 2022. | Series: AI for everything | Includes bibliographical references and index.
Identifiers: LCCN 2021042743 | ISBN 9781032052021 (hardback) | ISBN 9781032048291 (paperback) | ISBN 9781003196532 (ebook)
Subjects: LCSH: Sports--Data processing. | Sports--Mathematical models. | Artificial intelligence.
Classification: LCC GV706.8 .B728 2022 | DDC 796.02/1--dc23
LC record available at https://lccn.loc.gov/2021042743

ISBN: 978-1-032-05202-1 (hbk)
ISBN: 978-1-032-04829-1 (pbk)
ISBN: 978-1-003-19653-2 (ebk)

DOI: 10.1201/9781003196532

Typeset in Joanna
by Deanta Global Publishing Services, Chennai, India

Any opinions presented in this book are the personal views of the authors and do not necessarily reflect the official policies or positions of their organizations.

*In memory of Addie Brady who loved
to learn and would have loved to
have been involved with this book.*

– Chris

*To my lovely wife Marjolein and
children, Wout, Vincent and Arthur.
In loving memory of my father ir
Jan Tuyls, a role model for life.*

– Karl

*Dedicated to those who have
never had a book dedicated to
them, which (I think?) include
Leanne, Sara, Saied and Goli.*

– Shayegan

CONTENTS

ACKNOWLEDGMENTS

How do an Englishman, a Belgian, and a Canadian-Iranian meet and subsequently decide to jointly write a book on the vast possibilities that artificial intelligence creates for sports?

Coincidence? Serendipity? Readers can decide for themselves. Whatever it was, they formed a complementary team, sharing a vision of AI for Sports in the short, mid and long term.

Stanford, March 2018 – Karl and Shayegan meet at a spring symposium on Artificial Intelligence (AAAI). Research interests between both are well aligned, and in November 2018, Shayegan, an MIT graduate, joined Karl's Game Theory team at DeepMind.

Liverpool – London – Paris, November 2019 – Karl and Shayegan start up a research project on AI for Sports, in close collaboration with Liverpool Football Club, including various DeepMind researchers. Jointly they publish a paper on their work in the *Journal of Artificial Intelligence* in April 2020: "Game Plan: What AI Can Do for Football, and What Football Can Do for AI".

London – Paris (virtual), December 2020 – Thore Graepel introduces Karl to Elliott Morsia, commissioning editor for CRC Press & Routledge, to discuss the opportunity of writing a book with

Chris on the topic of AI for Sports. Karl and Elliott meet, and Elliott explains that Chris, who has a strong background in sports management, is looking for AI experts with interests in sports to join a new book project. Even though Karl only made his official decision to engage in the project early January 2021, he realized later that due to his initial conversations with Chris Brady in December 2020 the project had already started as of that first captivating conversation.

London – Paris (virtual), January 2021 – Karl who works intensively on AI for Sports with Shayegan realizes that the project would benefit substantially from including Shayegan as another AI expert and co-author of the project. On January 7 they meet for the first time with the three of them and shortly after the project officially takes off.

Merging together expertise in sports, sports management and business, with technical knowledge in artificial intelligence, supported by a joint network with stakeholders from various sports, digital technology and AI, is the unique combination that made this book possible.

Needless to say that we could not have written this book without the support and contributions of many people. Special thanks to our families and friends, for the countless hours we were spending together as authors, and consequently not with them. The input and critical thoughts of many people, with whom we had inspiring conversations, were indispensable in the writing process. These included, among many others, R. C. Buford (San Antonio Spurs), Thierry Geerts (country director Google Belgium), colleagues at DeepMind and Sportsology, editors and support staff at CRC Press & Routledge (Elliot Morsia, Talitha Duncan-Todd, Vijay Bose and Todd Perry).

Three strangers of different ages, different nationalities, different cultures and different disciplines meet, write a book and then depart as friends for life.

Thank you to everyone involved,

Chris, Karl and Shayegan

ABOUT THE AUTHORS

Professor Chris Brady is currently the Chief Intelligence Officer at Sportsology, a US-based consultancy to elite sports organizations across the globe. Professor Brady has had a varied working life, ranging from a line worker at Chrysler in Detroit in his teens to managing a bookmaker's shop, from a land surveyor to a semi-professional footballer, from a naval officer to a management consultant. Prior to joining Sportsology, he was most recently Professor of Management Studies at Salford University, where he founded the Centre for Sports Business, which focused on the production of high-quality research with a particular emphasis on statistical analytics and future trend analysis within the global sports industry.

Previously, Professor Brady was the Dean of BPP Business School, Dean of the Business School at Bournemouth University and Deputy Dean responsible for external affairs and business development at the Cass Business School (now Bayes Business School). He also served in the Royal Navy for 16 years, including appointments in the joint HQ intelligence cells during the first Gulf War and the Balkans crises.

He is the author of books and articles on subjects as varied as US foreign policy, British Cabinet government and business. Most recently he has co-authored the award-winning book *Quiet Leadership* with Carlo Ancelotti. His other books include the best-selling *The 90-Minute Manager*. He has also written on specific business issues in *The End of the Road*, the story of BMW's ownership of Rover and its aftermath; *The Extra Mile*, which deals with employee engagement; and *Intelligent M&A*, an analysis of the intelligence function within the M&A process.

Professor Brady is an advisor to the League Managers' Association's (LMA) Institute of Leadership and High Performance. He played, coached (UEFA 'A' license) and managed football semi-professionally throughout his working life and has also been qualified to coach tennis, squash and trampoline but admits that he probably draws most enjoyment from the movies and from football.

Karl Tuyls (FBCS) is a Team Lead at DeepMind, Paris, France; an Honorary Professor of Computer Science at the University of Liverpool, UK; and a Guest Professor at the University of Leuven, Belgium. Previously, he held academic positions at the Vrije Universiteit Brussel, Hasselt University, Eindhoven University of Technology and Maastricht University. Prof. Tuyls has received several awards with his research, including the Information Technology prize 2000 in Belgium, best demo award at AAMAS'12 and winner of various Robocup@Work competitions ('13, '14), and he was a co-author of the runner-up best paper award at ICML'18. Furthermore, his research has received substantial attention from national and international press and media, most recently his work on Sports Analytics featured in Wired UK. He is a fellow of the British Computer Society (BCS), is on the editorial board of the *Journal of Autonomous Agents and Multi-Agent Systems*, and is editor-in-chief of the Springer Briefs series on Intelligent Systems. Prof. Tuyls is also an emeritus member of the board of directors of the International Foundation for Autonomous Agents and Multiagent Systems.

Shayegan Omidshafiei is a senior research scientist in DeepMind's Game Theory team, where he also co-leads DeepMind's Sports Analytics effort. His research interests include multiagent systems, reinforcement learning, robotics and control systems. He previously received his Ph.D. at the Laboratory for Information and Decision Systems (LIDS) and Aerospace Controls Laboratory (ACL) at MIT. He received a B.A.Sc. degree from the University of Toronto in 2012 and an S.M. degree in Aeronautics and Astronautics from MIT in 2015. He is co-inventor of five patents filed with the United States Patent Office.

INTRODUCTION

> **Artificial intelligence (AI):** the study of machines or computational methods that can perceive, accrue knowledge and subsequently make decisions affecting a domain in a manner aligned to desired objectives.
>
> **Machine learning (ML):** a subfield of AI that involves machines that learn to make decisions using various perceptual experiences.

WHY NOW?

Because it feels like we are at a tipping point. The recent acceleration in the progress of artificial intelligence (AI) and machine learning has opened a wealth of potential analytics opportunities in both team and individual sports, and the story of AI in sports is also integral to the story of the relationship between humans and machines.

From the beginning of what became known as artificial intelligence in the mid-1950s, the link between games and sports has been fundamental as has the notion of sporting competition. This book

DOI: 10.1201/9781003196532-1

will explore how that link reached the place it occupies today, where we currently stand in the relationship and what the future may hold. Inevitably, it will also tend to focus on the competitive advantages (and disadvantages) that AI brings to the sporting ecosystem.

While the history of AI tends to be dated either from the late 1940s or from the first use of the term by John McCarthy, an American computer scientist, in 1955, the history of the relationship between humans and machines and, indeed sport, can be dated in millennia. Although the main focus of the book is at the development of the human–machine interface from those early conversations about thinking machines in the 1940s/1950s, the history of how humans and machines have interacted in previous millennia is also significant and dealt with in the early part of the book. The history, the current state and the potential futures of AI and Sport are, therefore, presented by mapping the journey of AI in sport within the narrative of the human–machine interface.

While we were contemplating how to open this book, two separate events occurred, which in our view confirmed what should be a predominant theme of the book, namely, the relationships between humans and machines and the symbiotic enhancement of the lives of both and how that relationship plays out in the sporting arena. The first event was the successful landing of the *Perseverance* spacecraft on the surface of Mars.[1] In the excitement of the moment, a NASA employee told TV audiences that it was a perfect example of the potential of how machine and human intelligences could interact to achieve great things.[2] Incidentally, who else but a human could be bothered to work out the naming of the central AI program in such a way that the acronym for the program would be MAARS, the machine learning-based Analytics for Autonomous Rover Systems.

The second relevant event was the publication of the latest novel by the Nobel Prize winner, Kazuo Ishiguro, entitled, *Klara and the Sun*.[3] Klara, the narrator, is an Artificial Friend (AF), a human-like robot designed to be a child's companion. She sits in the window of a shop waiting to be bought while observing human nature based on the myriad passing footfall of human shoppers. She learns from the humans while simultaneously providing her human contacts with insights into themselves.

Despite the gentle tone of the book and the benign sense of Klara as an "intelligent friend", Ishiguro imbues his story with an almost subliminal fear that AI had the capability to also be an enabler of the "*centralization of power and be dangerously seductive*". However, concerns aside, he remains hopeful and still sees the future as a "*celebration of the synergy between the best of humans and machines*".[4]

Both the Mars landing and the Ishiguro novel are indicative of the centrality of the place that Artificial intelligence has taken in our collective utopian and/or dystopian views of our current situation and our possible futures. Whether AI is or will become a positive, negative or neutral influence, there is no doubt that it is increasingly driving the present, and, as Cade Metz of Wired has said, "*the ideas driving [AI] are going to drive our future*". Ishiguro tacitly forces us to face the possibility that human life may not be unique and the manner in which humans learn and their relationship with learning machines needs to be at the heart of the development of AI.

A United Nations report in 2019 believed that in the near future

> the way we learn, access knowledge … will no longer be the same. From now on, the acquisition of digital skills stands at the centre of all our education programmes … we must 'learn to learn' because the pace of innovation is rapidly transforming [the way we live].[5]

If what and how we learn is the key to human advancement, then the relationship between humans and machines that learn will inevitably develop at an ever-increasing pace.

Since the 1940s, when the idea of "thinking machines" first seemed to be a realistic aspiration, theories have tended to outpace the practical implementation of those theories, mostly hampered by the inability of the technology to keep pace with the ideas. In 2021, the technology has closed the gap with the theory considerably.

When McCarthy first used the term "artificial intelligence", he did so as an umbrella term to encourage interdisciplinary research into the notion of a "thinking machine", a single discipline that had not really developed since Alan Turing's original question, "*Can machines think?*" in 1950. In 2021, enormous processing power is helping technology to be a peer of the theory, and disciplinary boundaries are, or should be, less inhibiting. However, close to 70 years after Turing's question, we are still debating the answer.

In fact, Turing himself very quickly conceded that it was an "absurd" question and instead decided to reformulate the question in the form of a game, "the imitation game".[6] From the outset, therefore, games have had a special place in the story of artificial intelligence. Despite his concern about the absurdity of his own question, Turing nevertheless answers it by stating later in that original article, that he believed,

> that in fifty years' time it will be possible to program computers ... to make them play the imitation game so well that an average interrogator will not have more than 70 percent chance of making the right identification after five minutes of questioning.

Artificial intelligence is here to stay, and the way in which it impacts human existence will be profound. Through our analysis of AI in sports, we want this book to add value to the technological, theoretical and even ethical conversations that lay ahead.

WHY SPORTS?

Because sports and competition are inherent in the human condition – we play games, we compete. When interviewed after the publication of DeepMind's *AlphaFold* project in *Nature*, Demis Hassabis (DeepMind's founder and CEO) stated that,

> What's amazing to me is that this thesis that I had when I started DeepMind – build AI, **prove it on games**, then when we've done

that, to use it on these difficult scientific problems – seems to be working.[7] [emphasis added]

In doing so, he was tacitly acknowledging that a portal through which to advance AI was presented by the structures and complexities of human game playing – sports.

While chatbots may have ostensibly passed the Turing Test, as the imitation game came to be called, we are still unable to answer the question as to whether a machine can actually understand human meaning and can subsequently learn from that meaning simply through observation and then, as a consequence of that learning, solve our human problems. That sequence will inevitably happen, and in the process, AI will continue to change the world around us on a daily basis, and that applies to the sporting world probably more than most. Not least because, as the industrial deployment of AI enables more leisure time, sports and games will only grow in societal significance from an already powerful base level.

The idea of machine-enhanced control of human action is not new, and it has been a dream in professional sport from the moment the notion of coaching first emerged. Indeed, in 1970, Bill McGarry, the then manager of English first division (equivalent to today's Premier League) team Wolverhampton Wanderers, wired up his youth team players with a simple walkie-talkie connection in an experiment during a match and coached the players individually in real time. Probably, as a result of its success, the English Football Association immediately banned the practice. However, the dream lives on in the mind of every sports coach – to be able to affect their players and the game in real time.

As the exponential progress in processing power and understanding of machine learning is likely to accelerate even further, this is an opportune time in which to take stock of the roles that AI plays and can and will play in the present and future of sports. Some of the greatest strides in AI in general have been through its relationship with games. Furthermore, its continued application to sports and competition will simultaneously add value to our understanding of machine learning.

Football (soccer)[8] in particular is seen as a fertile ground for both the game itself and the advancement of AI for various reasons. In comparison to some other sports, football started rather late with systematically collecting large sets of data. This has a number of specific causes, such as the far less controllable settings of the game in comparison to other sports (e.g. large outdoor pitch, dynamic game play etc.), and the dominant *credo* in football, to rely mainly on human specialists with track records and experience in professional football.

Football analytics brings forth many technological challenges that are well suited to be tackled by a wide variety of AI techniques. Football provides a great laboratory of a real-world setting where the intersection of three fields – computer vision, statistical learning and game theory – can be analyzed. It is where players need to take sequential decisions in the presence of other players (cooperative and adversarial) and as such game theory, a theory of interactive decision-making, becomes highly relevant. Moreover, tactical solutions for particular in-game situations can be learnt based on in-game and specific player representations, which also makes statistical learning a highly relevant area. Finally, players can be tracked, and game scenarios can be recognized automatically from widely available image and video inputs.

The authors therefore apologize, in advance, if our case studies disproportionately reference football. Naturally, other team sports such as Gridiron football, baseball, cricket, rugby, boxing, ice hockey and basketball will be addressed, as will predominantly individual sports such as cycling, golf, gymnastics and boxing, in addition to hybrids such as team cycling.

Similarly, we will look at the fan experience and the commercial potential for the use of AI. On-field performance, entertainment and commercial imperatives are interdependent, and AI will clearly have a major effect on the entire sporting ecosystem. Our task is to examine the past and present manifestations of AI within the sporting context and to imagine the future it will have both in and upon sport.

Finally, we note that the speed of innovation in the sporting domain demands that ethical considerations cannot be ignored, and they will be addressed. An increasing number of research groups and cross-organizational consortia are driving discussions and conducting analyses of relevant ethical aspects of AI research. Such efforts are, of course, especially important given the increasing prospect of AI advancements having widespread impacts on day-to-day lives. The acknowledgment of the powerful role that sport plays societally gives increased significance to the ethical discourse around AI for sports.

NOTES

1. https://www.nasa.gov/perseverance/
2. "*Dare mighty things*", was the text written in binary on the Perseverance Rover's parachute as it landed: https://mars.nasa.gov/resources/25646/mars-decoder-ring/
3. Coincidentally, Klara was also the name of the wife of the game theorist, John von Neumann, with whom Alan Turing shared time at Princeton's famed Institute for Advanced Study.
4. BBC TV interview 1 March 2021.
5. United Nations (2019). *Towards an Ethics of Artificial Intelligence* | United Nations. [online] Available at: https://www.un.org/en/chronicle/article/towards-ethics-artificial-intelligence
6. A.M. Turing, Computing Machinery and Intelligence, *Mind*, LIX, 236, October 1950, 433–60, https://doi.org/10.1093/mind/LIX.236.433
7. https://www.nature.com/articles/d41586-020-03348-4
8. Throughout this book, the term "football" will be used interchangeably with "soccer" to refer to Association Football. Other forms of football (e.g. Gridiron) will be referred to as a specific genre.

Part 1

HOW DID WE GET TO WHERE WE ARE?

1

BEFORE TURING (PRE-1950)

There is a long history of interaction between humans and machines. Indeed, evidence that the abacus was in use more than 5,000 years ago proves the human fascination with computation may well be innate. Throughout the 17th century, Schickard, Oughtred, Pascal and Leibniz all developed versions of what might generically be referred to as calculating or computing machines. The construction of Wolfgang von Kempelen's Mechanical Turk for the amusement of the court of Maria Theresa of Austria was also indicative of the human fascination with the idea of machines that could think and as such could outplay humans at their own games. In the case of the Turk, that game was chess. The fact that the "machine" was a fake with a human chess master hidden inside is another story.

There is also a long history of chess-playing automatons up to and including IBM's Deep Blue taking on and beating Gary Kasparov in 1997. Zermelo's 1913 paper[1] showing that chess is determinate was an early example of a game-theoretic approach, which eventually led to machines such as Deep Blue. Incidentally, more recently, Amazon has created its own Mechanical Turk (Mturk), a crowdsourcing marketplace that ironically enables companies to find and recruit human beings.[2] It's not clear how long Amazon's Mturk will be useful, but it will do well to outlast the fake Turk which survived

DOI: 10.1201/9781003196532-3

for 84 years after its creation in 1770 until its demise in a fire in Philadelphia in 1854.

The 19th century saw further advances through such work as Babbage's Analytical Engine, a proposed design for a mechanical computer, arguably the first general-purpose computing device. One of Babbage's attendees at his regular soirees, Ada Lovelace, is often credited as the world's first computer programmer as a result of developing an expertise in the use of punched cards to sequence instructions for how the Analytical Engine could be programmed. As early as 1843, she published a paper which concluded that there was a critical distinction between the Analytical Engine and the existing calculators of the time. When the second Tuesday in October comes round, be sure to celebrate Ada Lovelace Day, a day dedicated to the contributions of women to science, technology, engineering and mathematics.

Babbage's work and that of Boole and Lovelace presaged what might be termed the first computational machine, invented by Herman Hollerith in the 1880s using an advanced punched card system. While working at the Massachusetts Institute of Technology, Hollerith created a machine that enabled information to be converted into electrical impulses by way of a system of punched holes, originally on strips of paper but eventually on cards. The Hollerith "punched card" system was used to mechanize the laborious task of number crunching for the 1890 census in the United States. At the time it was said to have saved the government in the region of $5 million (close to $150 million in today's currency) by enabling the collection, collation and analysis of the census data, all to be completed by a fraction of the labor force in a fraction of the time. This basic design would provide the foundation blocks of the computing industry well into the 20th century, often driven by the company that Hollerith founded, which eventually morphed into the International Business Machines Corporation (IBM).

There is also a rich history of the relationship of humans with games. Indeed, Johan Huizinga argued in his 1938 book, Homo Ludens ("man as a game player" being a reasonable translation) that games are so fundamental to the human condition that they were a necessary condition for the development of human cultures. For Huizinga, games necessarily preceded the evolution of all complex human activities.

It is almost certain that game playing has existed from the earliest human communities. One of its earliest manifestations being as a training activity for war fighting purposes, which just as quickly evolved into sports and sporting events such as the Olympics or jousting competitions. There is also considerable evidence that all ancient civilizations engaged in bat (stick) and ball games, which, while they may train hand/eye coordination, seem to have been for pure enjoyment.

While such sporting games satisfied the training needs of the front-line soldier, it was left to board games such as the ancient Greek game of Petteia (a draughts/checkers type game) and chess to begin to educate the military at what was perceived as a strategic level; indeed Chaturanga, the ancient Indian predecessor of chess, derives its etymology from the phrase "four members" or "limbs", referring to the respective branches of the military at the time: infantry, cavalry, chariotry and elephantry. Interestingly, as wargaming developed as a specific discipline, dice were used to add the randomness that occurs in the reality of war, akin to the randomness that exists in all sporting activities. Throughout the 19th century, nations began developing war games largely derived from what is often considered to be the precursor of all war games, the Prussian kriegsspiel.

This early war game was initially created by a Prussian nobleman, George Leopold von Reisswitz, and later developed by his son, Georg Heinrich Rudolf Johann von Reisswitz, in 1824. The game was copied by many other national militaries, particularly in the years between the First and Second World Wars, including the United States and Japan who scenario-planned war in the Pacific, which essentially played out as both sides had predicted in the war games. Sadly, the war gamers had not predicted that humans would ignore the lessons these games were delivering and continued with their plans irrespective of the most obvious outcomes.

What starts as practicing for a specific need such as soldiering soon develops into games and ultimately into formalized sporting activity. In much the same way, the analytical aspects of war soon became crucial in games and eventually to organized sports also. It was in the mid-19th century that one of the earliest manifestations of a more analytical approach to sport emerged with the creation of baseball's "box score" by Henry Chadwick. It was an early attempt to summarize players' achievements in baseball games, similar to cricket scorecards of the same era. It listed games played and the number of outs, runs, home runs and strikeouts. The results of Chadwick's efforts were first published in an article in an 1859 edition of the weekly news sheet, *The New York Clipper*. That original box score card was reprinted in 1925 in an article in *Baseball Magazine* (Figure 1.1).

Chadwick was inducted into the Baseball Hall of Fame in 1938, and in 2009, the Society for American Baseball Research (SABR) created the Henry Chadwick Award for outstanding contributions by baseball researchers. One recipient of that award is Bill James, of whom, more later.

Fifty years after Chadwick's Clipper article, Hugh Fullerton and John J. Evers' published another seminal work on baseball, *Touching*

The First Recorded Box Score of a Ball Game

STARS	R	H	P	A	E	EXCELSIORS	R	H	P	A	E
Tracy, c	1	0	8	0	3	Reynolds, ss	1	2	1	3	1
F. Whitney, 1b	2	2	5	2	0	E. Whitney, 3b	2	1	1	3	1
E. Patchen, rf	3	2	1	0	0	Legget, c	3	2	8	1	2
S. Patchen, ss	3	2	1	3	1	Pearsall, 1b	1	0	7	0	0
Fairbanks, cf	2	1	0	0	1	C. Whiting, cf	1	1	2	1	0
Ticknor, 2b	2	1	5	0	1	Brainard, 2b	1	1	3	0	1
Creighton, P.	1	0	4	1	0	Polhemus, rf	1	1	2	0	1
Manly, 3b	1	1	1	1	1	Markham, lf	0	0	2	0	0
Flanly, lf	2	2	2	0	0	Etheridge, P.	2	2	1	2	1
Totals	17	11	27	7	7	Totals	12	10	27	10	4

Stars .... 2 0 3 0 1 0 1 0 10—17
Excelsiors ... 0 2 0 1 0 0 6 3—12
Earned runs—Stars 3, Excelsiors 2.

Battery errors—Stars 5, Excelsiors 4.
Struck out—Stars 1. Umpire, S. O'Brien
Time, 3 hours.

444

Figure 1.1 Henry Chadwick's first 'box score card' (Courtesy of the National Baseball Hall of Fame)

Second: The Science of Baseball, in which they statistically analyzed the 1909 season, and the game in general. Their aim, apart from just recording the 1909 season, was to

> assist "fans", younger ball players and all lovers of baseball to a better appreciation of the finer points of the national game and enable them to see behind the moves of the men on the field, the generalship and brainwork of "inside play".[3]

Despite the authors' rather grandiose claims for the game of baseball itself ("the game is the most highly developed, scientific and logical form of athletic pastime evolved by man"), the main thrust of their vision was to develop, perhaps without realizing it, a generic understanding of games. They believed that

> the game is the only one played which is founded upon exact and scientific lines. The playing field is laid out with such geometrical exactness … [to create] the ultimate evolution of the one universal game.[4]

The comprehensive nature of the book is clear from its contents page as shown in Figure 1.2.

Returning to the role that wargaming played in the development of games themselves, the end of the Second World War saw a resurgence of such activities as the US began scenario planning the thermonuclear war that its strategists believed to be inevitable. Scenario planning, like wargaming, is one of many ways of trying to predict the future or getting as close to it as possible for strategic, tactical, and/or operational reasons. The power of effective scenario planning, even more generally, lies in the fact that it taps into two of our most fundamental drivers – we are simultaneously *homo narrans* (humans as storytellers) and *homo ludens* (humans as game players). Scenario planning is essentially a story-telling and creative game playing process.

In a corporate sense, scenario planning as a discipline evolved seriously in the bowels of the newly formed RAND Corporation in

LIST OF CHAPTERS

Figure 1.2 The contents page of *Touching Second: The Science of Baseball* by Hugh Fullerton and John J. Evers

the early post–Second World War years. The heavyweight in that group, both physically and intellectually, was Herman Kahn, who later founded the Hudson Institute.[5] Kahn was one of the first to be labelled as a "futurist" and worked with such intellectual giants as the *Financial Times*' "Man of the Century", John von Neumann, one of the godfathers of game theory. Khan himself is often referred to as the father of scenario planning.[6]

Such men were at the forefront of the Cold War and had to concern themselves with thinking the unthinkable. Their job was to game a nuclear war: how to stop one; and if not, how to win one; and if not, how to survive one. In simple terms, they had to create stories about a future that few had contemplated. What was created at RAND complied with the first rule of scenario planning – the acceptance of a diversity of intellects. According to the *New Yorker*, they created an

> atmosphere that was one-part Southern California nonconformity and two parts University of Chicago rigor. People at RAND imagined themselves to be well out on the curve. They read widely and held salons, where they talked futurology .... They were eggheads in a world of meatheads, and they regarded the uniformed military man in the same way that the baseball statistician Bill James regarded Don Zimmer: as a relic of the pre-scientific dark ages, when the wisdom of experience passed for strategic thought.[7]

THE THEORY OF GAMES AND SPORT

Game theory is a theory of interactive decision-making that provides a toolbox for agents (or players) involved in an interaction to understand the behavior of others and choose the right actions in response to that same behavior. For a long time, game theory has been an academic endeavor of mathematicians and economists who studied games as an abstract mathematical construct, initially predominantly in zero-sum settings (what is won by one player must be lost by another), but later also in broader settings referred to as general-sum games. In the 1970s, game theory found its way to other fields, such as biology and sociology, with the introduction of evolutionary game theory by Maynard-Smith, for example. More recently, game-theoretic concepts are being applied in increasingly broader real-world settings, such as auctions, robotics and finance. As such, the "gamification" of concrete problems has taken off.

In this context, it is no surprise that these game-theoretic notions have also found their way into sports, where several of the core properties initially studied in abstract games also clearly come to the surface (cooperation, competition, incomplete information on the actions and intentions of other players etc.), which brings into focus the crucial role played by John von Neumann in understanding the relationship between AI and the sports ecosystem.

Although von Neumann's most recognized contribution is through the publication of *The Theory of Games and Economic Behavior*,[8] with his co-author Oskar Morgenstern in 1944, von Neumann's academic interest in games had begun nearly 20 years earlier. In the mid-1920s, discourse around the mathematics of games was burgeoning in eastern Europe, mostly among German and Hungarian academics and often based on Zermelo's theories concerning mathematics and the game of chess.[9]

Von Neumann always acknowledged his debt to Zermelo and also to the contemporaneous work of Emile Borel. As early as 1921, Borel had already published on the theory of games using, as would von Neumann, poker as his lab rat of choice. For both men, it was the element of bluffing and second-guessing the opponent within an environment of imperfect information that intrigued them. Borel even foresaw its use in both economic and military problem-solving.

While von Neumann and others worked on the relationship between set theory and "parlor games", von Neumann also recognized that there should be universality in their findings. As he stated,

> any event – given the external conditions and the participants in the situation … may be regarded as a game of strategy if one looks at the effect it has on the participants.

His argument was that it would be a more realistic and recognizable model than *homo economicus*, a theoretical construct that assumes humans as perfectly rational decision-makers.

Those early findings eventually spawned *The Theory of Games* in 1944, a year or so after von Neumann had joined a band of intellectual giants based at Los Alamos, New Mexico. This was the work that effectively established game theory as a genuine research field in its own right, extending von Neumann's earlier minimax theorem to games involving more than two players, and formally considering imperfect information games – such as poker.

Three years later, another cross-disciplinary research field was established when Norbert Wiener published *Cybernetics: or Control and Communication in the Animal and the Machine*.[10] Wiener, apparently unaware of André-Marie Ampère's earlier use of the term in his "Essai sur la philosophie des sciences", coined the word "cybernetics" to define his work as focusing on a theory of information processing and control. He realized that intelligent behavior resulted from a process of "feedback mechanisms", which would underpin the new discipline. If that were true, he reasoned, then such feedback processes could be emulated by machines. A further step toward the development of modern AI was the creation of *The Logic Theorist* program. Designed by Newell and Simon in 1955, it may well be considered the first AI program.

As with von Neumann's group at *Princeton's Institute of Advanced Study*, Wiener's collaborators, primarily Arturo Rosenblueth and Julian Bigelow, consisted of an eclectic group from a variety of established fields, effectively creating new disciplines in what Wiener describes as "the no-man's land between the various established fields". To believe that von Neumann or Wiener created these new fields alone would be unfair to the groups with which they both worked. The eclectic composition of the groups was as important, if not more so, as each individual within them. As Wiener explained,

> A proper exploration of these blank spaces on the map of science could only be made by a team ... each a specialist in his own field but each possessing a thoroughly sound and trained acquaintance with the fields of his neighbor's; all in the habit of working together, of knowing one another's intellectual customs, and of recognizing the significance of a colleague's new suggestion before it had taken on a full formal expression.

If AI winters[11] would later inhibit the progress of the discipline over the decades, then the 1950s must surely be seen as the AI spring, a time when solid foundations were laid. The year of 1950 alone produced such seminal works as Nash's distinction between cooperative and non-cooperative games, and the Nash equilibrium published in his doctoral dissertation, "Non-Cooperative Games". 1950 was also the year when Alan Turing proposed the imitation game as a measure of machine intelligence, as well as when a paper by Claude Shannon, an engineer-mathematician out of the MIT stable, analyzed chess and demonstrated how a computer could be used to play the game. As Shannon explained, his paper was

> concerned with the problem of constructing a computing routine or "program" for a modern general purpose computer which will enable it to play chess. Although perhaps of no practical importance, the question is of theoretical interest, and it is hoped that a satisfactory solution of this problem will act as a wedge in attacking other problems of a similar nature and of greater significance.[12]

His concepts still play a central role in large parts of what constitutes the AI research domain.

NOTES

1. E. Zermelo, On the Application of Set Theory to the Theory of Chess Games, Proceedings of the Fifth International Congress of Mathematicians, Cambridge, 22–28 Aug. 1912, 1913, II, pp. 501–4. Also, "On an Application of Set Theory to the Theory of the Game of Chess" in Rasmusen E., ed., 2001. Readings in Games and Information, Wiley-Blackwell, pp. 79–82.
2. Amazon Mechanical Turk (mturk.com).
3. J. Evers, and H. Fullerton, Touching Second: The Science of Baseball, 1910 (Introduction).
4. Ibid, p. 12.
5. The Hudson Institute challenges conventional thinking and helps manage strategic transitions to the future through interdisciplinary studies in defense, international relations, economics, health care, technology, culture and law. https://www.hudson.org/
6. Peter Schwartz, The Art of the Long View: Planning for the Future in an Uncertain World, New York: Currency Doubleday, 1991, p. 7.

7. The New Yorker, June 27, 2005 Issue, *Fat Man, Herman Kahn and the Nuclear Age* by Louis Menand.

8. J. Von Neumann, and O. Morgenstern, *The Theory of Games and Economic Behavior*, Princeton, NJ: Princeton U. Press, [1944] 1947.

9. E. Zermelo, *On the Application of Set Theory to the Theory of Chess games*, Proceedings of the Fifth International Congress of Mathematicians, Cambridge, 22–28 Aug. 1912, 1913, II, pp. 501–4.

10. N. Wiener, *Cybernetics: or Control and Communication in the Animal and the Machine*, Wiley, 1948.

11. An AI winter was a period in which research into the topic was strangled, usually as a result of over-hyping the potential of the discipline at that time.

12. C. Shannon, Programming a Computer for Playing Chess, *Philosophical Magazine*, Ser.7, 41, 314, March 1950, XXII.

2

THE SPORTS ANALYST COMETH

In 1951 came what is generally regarded as the first notational system in football. A serving officer in the Royal Air Force, Wing Commander Charles Reep, developed his system almost as a hobby. Reep is often a significant omission from the history of football management, whereas he should be seen as a pioneer rather than the radical outsider he was deemed to be during his lifetime. Early in 1950, Reep appeared on the scene as possibly the advanced party for the arrival of Billy Beane (of *Moneyball* fame) and other acolytes in more recent times. Very quickly Reep became the *bête noire* of the beautiful game, described by journalist Brian Glanville as the leader of "a fanatical credo, a pseudo-religion" or by the more prosaic Michael Henderson as one of the *50 People Who Fouled Up Football*.[1]

In reality, he was nothing of the sort; rather he was the first genuine data analyst to bother to turn his attention to the production of valuable data for use by football's domain specialists – the managers and coaches. It is said that the time, date and place that the new role of the sports analyst was born occurred,

> at 15.50 on 18 March 1950, when [Reep] a spectator at Swindon Town's home game against Bristol Rovers took a pencil and notebook out of his pocket. Wing Commander Charles Reep was at that moment beginning to create the first comprehensive notational analysis system for football.[2]

DOI: 10.1201/9781003196532-4

Reep met Stan Cullis, the manager of Wolves, shortly after England's Wembley debacle in 1953 at the hands of the rampant Hungarian national team. Cullis had been impressed with the work done by Reep with Brentford, where he had helped them avoid relegation in the previous season. Reep was asked to advise on Cullis' obsession with debunking the hype around the "Hungarian style". Cullis wanted to retain the English style of more direct back to front passing while also learning about the more intricate methods of the Hungarians.

Cullis used many of Reep's findings while developing tactics to beat the Hungarian champion club side, Honved Budapest, when they came to Wolverhampton in the following December. Wolves won 3–2 after being 2–0 down early in the game. However, the victory may well have had more to do with smart tactics than data analysis. The story goes that Cullis ordered the pitch to be heavily watered at half time to slow down the speedy and intricate passing game of the Hungarians; three Wolves' goals followed in the second half.

Reep retired from the RAF a year later and subsequently spent three years as a performance analyst for Sheffield Wednesday. Reep's military background was (and still is) often ridiculed within the professional game, yet it was an environment where he could refine his theories on the back of huge datasets. He was often in charge of military representative teams which he used as subjects for analysis and tactical experimentation away from the pressures of a fully professional situation. As an obituary article explained:

> Reep is clearly the first person to develop and apply a sports notational system in this country. His work in the 1950s predates, by perhaps two decades, subsequent attempts to notate and analyse performance in football.[3]

During his annotation of more than 2,000 games, all using simple pen and paper records, he established several "rules", including the "3-pass optimization rule", which was later criticized for generating a more direct style of play that was anathema to the football purists.

As with most statistical analyses, many flaws tend to be in the interpretation and practices drawn from that analysis, rather than the statistical outputs themselves. Reep's "bête noire" sobriquet was unnecessarily harsh.

The mid-1950s saw further advances and, indeed, the first mention of the term *Artificial Intelligence* (AI) at a Dartmouth College summer conference organized predominantly by John McCarthy and ably assisted by Claude Shannon, Marvin Minsky and Nathan Rochester. This conference is now widely considered to be the event that confirmed AI as a distinct research field.

Toward the end of the decade, McCarthy left Dartmouth and linked up with Minsky at MIT and the pair founded the MIT Artificial Intelligence Laboratory (AI Lab). In 1963, MIT pulled the AI Lab together with the Laboratory for Computer Science (LCS), a US Defense Department–sponsored enterprise, together morphing into the Computer Science and Artificial Intelligence Laboratory (CSAIL). In 2021, CSAIL has nearly a thousand researchers working with an annual budget close to $70 million.[4]

Others from the 1950s who deserve honorable mention include cyberneticians such as Warren McCulloch and Walter Pitts (introducing the first artificial model of a neuron, the "perceptron", in the 1940s) and perhaps more significantly for the development of AI, Newell, Simon and Shaw, who jointly created the *Logic Theorist* computer program in 1956 during their time together at the RAND Corporation. Herbert Simon was one of the genuine polymaths of the 20th century, while Allen Newell and Cliff Shaw were the technocrats responsible for the programming and coding.

The logic theory machine was originally programmed to derive proofs of logic expressions in Russell and Whitehead's *Principia Mathematica* and is claimed by many to be the first AI program. Newell and Simon later created the *General Problem Solver*, a program which incorporated the centrality of the feedback principle proposed by Norbert Wiener in *Cybernetics*. Interestingly, Newell also worked as a research assistant for Oskar Morgenstern. And the connections just keep on coming.

The AI Spring continued into the 1960s, especially for the relationship between AI and sport. In 1964, Earnshaw Cook published his book, *Percentage Baseball*, in which he conducted a mathematical analysis of baseball. In one sense, Cook's can be seen as the first sabermetrics volume, even before the term was in the language. An early first edition of the book now resides in the permanent collection of the National Baseball Hall of Fame and Museum in Cooperstown, New York. Cook was an engineering professor at Johns Hopkins University and was nicknamed the "slide rule" professor after the publication of the book. He wanted the book to be for

> those aficionados of percentage baseball who have managed to retain vestigial recollections of freshman mathematics. In a small concession to sanity, many derivations and calculations have been relegated to separate tables as less to interfere with continuity of discussion. The argument is not difficult but it is complicated because baseball is an exceedingly intricate game.[5]

Cook traced his book's origins to a coffee table debate with a friend about the value, or otherwise, of the sacrifice bunt. Three years of research later and the book arrived. Sixty years later and the debate about the value of the bunt continues.

In a 1964 *Sports Illustrated* interview with Cook, the renowned sports journo Frank Deford explained how Cook

> was amused that [baseball] was still played more traditionally than realistically …. He was astonished that nobody had figured it out before him.

However, not everybody was spellbound by Cook's analysis. Bill James, of "sabermetrics" fame, wrote in his 1981 *Baseball Abstract*,

> Cook knew everything about statistics and nothing at all about baseball— and for that reason, all of his answers are wrong, all of his methods useless.

Bill James himself describes sabermetrics as "the search for objective knowledge about baseball". The stereotypical descriptions of Cook and James as the opposite ends of a spectrum between only numbers at one end and only experience at the other are wide of the mark. It nevertheless serves as a proxy for a lot of the friction between the scientists and the domain specialists.

THE CYBERNETICIANS JOIN THE PARTY

An early milestone in cybernetics for sports occurred in 1965 with the inaugural (they hoped) USSR Conference on "Cybernetics and Sport" held at the Soviet Order of Lenin Institute of Physical Education in Moscow. The concept was to invite as many scientific disciplines to be represented at the conference as possible, in the spirit of cognitive diversity established by the elite groups at Princeton, MIT, Harvard and RAND in the early postwar years. It was not, therefore, without its propaganda value to the relatively new communist state. Thematically, it was to focus on the application of mathematical analyses of the management of sports activities. The main topics would be:

- Research and mathematical modeling of physiological processes during muscle activity;
- Simulation of the physical condition in athletes (assessment of fitness);
- Modeling of training processes;
- Simulation of sports activities;
- Methods of collecting and processing data in the process of performing sports exercises.

In general, the conference was a success with over 700 attendees and some valuable papers delivered.

A second conference did take place in 1968. Attendance had shrunk to just over 100, but that still represented 39 separate disciplines from 27 cities, and a further 38 papers delivered in the following categories:

- General theoretical aspects of the use of computers in sports;
- Multivariate statistical analysis of research results in sports;
- Usage of computers to solve biomedical problems.

While the conference itself may not have come up to the expectations of the organizers, it nevertheless demonstrated the continuing importance of "mathematization" in scientific research, both in the theory and in the practice of sports. As the papers of both conferences were delivered in Russian, they did not gain the attention they might otherwise have expected or deserved. Perhaps the most interesting consensus to come out of the conferences was the general agreement

> that it is impossible to fully replace teachers and coaches [with] cybernetic tools.[6]

Notwithstanding the potential for hyperbole on the part of the Soviet authorities, there had been, in parallel with the development of cybernetics in the West, a strong presence in the Russian scientific community of an interest in the significance of feedback in both human and machine systems. In the 19th century, for example, the mathematician Ivan Vyshnegradsky proposed a theory of the autonomous control of systems fundamentally reliant on feedback.

Similarly, Ivan Pavlov's work on autonomous reflexes in the 1920s and 1930s is said to have been impactful upon Norbert Wiener, whose student, Stafford Beer, in turn, further elaborated the centrality of feedback in the human nervous system in his work on Systems Theory.[7] All of these were prerequisites for the foundational principle of cybernetics: regulation through feedback.

In 1955–1956, a seminar series on cybernetics was started at Moscow University, but it was not until Wieners' book was published in Russian in 1968 that cybernetics was fully cemented as a dominant discipline within the Soviet scientific establishment. The battle between the Pavlovian reflex theorists and the Soviet "cybernetic physiologists" that had raged in the 1950s as a clash of opposing man/machine metaphors appeared to have been resolved in favor of the cyberneticians.

One of the beneficiaries of that victory was the *Dnipropetrovsk Institute of Physical Science* in Ukraine, one of the earliest cybernetic institutes in the USSR which had opened in 1957. Coincidentally, in 1968, a recently retired Ukrainian player began his football coaching career at *Dnipro Dnipropetrovsk*, a team located near the Institute. That player was Valerij Lobanovskyj. Lobanovskyj, himself a gifted schoolboy mathematician, was intrigued by the work being carried out at the Institute. He sought out and met the Dean, Anatolij Zelentsov, and the two men immediately became friends.

The significance of cybernetics for sports coaches is that it provides the perfect discipline within which to study the complexity of a game such as football, which many still argue cannot be fully analyzed. As Wiener explains, systems require control and communication to operate efficiently, and it is that necessity around which the minds of Lobanovskyj and Zelentsov met. They formed the perfect team to adopt a scientific approach to football centered on the developing discipline of cybernetics. Lobanovskyj accepted the systems theoretical convention that for one system (a team) to control another system (an opposing team), it had to be able to control the complexity of the situation within an environment (the game) better than its opponent, and that the key to such control was communication and feedback.

As Lobanovskyj and Zelentsov explained it in their article, "The Methodological Basis of the Development of Training Models",

the first thing we have in mind is to strive for new courses of action that will not allow the opponent to adapt to our style of play. If an opponent has adjusted himself to our style of play and found a counter play, then we need to find a new strategy. That is the dialectic of the game. You have to go forward in such a way and with such a range of attacking options that it will force the opponent to make a mistake. In other words, it's necessary to force the opponent into the condition you want them to be in. One of the most important means of doing that is to vary the size of the playing area.

The two men began to test their theories at Dnipro, which immediately bore fruit, if not silverware, at the time. Lobanovskyj would raise questions for Zelentsov to answer and to subsequently create innovative models derived from his answers. The result was a Dnepr team that for three years became a beacon for new ideas throughout Soviet football.

In 1973, Lobanovskyj moved to Dinamo Kiev, where his greatest triumphs would occur. At Kiev, Lobanovskyj and Zelentsov were able to not only develop their ideas but also to build state-of-the-art facilities to enable the implementation of those ideas. No detail was too small to be considered for its competitive advantage. Zelentsov explains that they would even go to the local theater to watch the Ukrainian director Georgi Tovstonogov, just to see "how the future show is 'modelled'".[8]

They also studied, and copied, the flight patterns of bees. Zelentsov explains,

> Have you seen how bees fly? A hive is in the air, and someone is the leader. It turns right and all the hive turns right. It turns left and all the hive turns left. The same is in football. There is a leader who takes a decision to move, say, here. The rest need to correct their motion following the leader…. Every team has players which [enable] coalitions, every team has players which destroy them. The first are called to create on the field, the latter – to destroy the team actions of opponents.[9]

Anyone involved in coaching football would understand the connection between the actions of the bees and the actions of the first player to engage with the opposition, or ball, "triggering" the subsequent actions of their teammates. Lobanovskyj has been described as the "iron curtain's Billy Beane". Billy Beane would almost certainly agree that it is actually he who is Oakland's Lobanovskyj.

WINTER'S HERE

Shortly after Lobanovskyj's arrival at Dnipro, Marvin Minsky and Seymour Papert published a book, *Perceptrons*, which included a stinging critique highlighting the limitations of the perceptrons-based framework. Arguably, some of the views expressed in their book contributed to the first AI winter, a period where funding for AI research dried up significantly and funding for continuing research into artificial neural networks virtually came to a halt. It would be another decade before that research made a conservative comeback.

Prior to Minsky and Papert's book, the American psychologist Frank Rosenblatt had received considerable funding from the US Office of Naval Research, one result of which was his creation of the *perceptron* algorithm, similar in form to a *logistic linear regression*. Initial results were promising since the first hardware implementation of the algorithm, called the Mark I Perceptron machine, was able to demonstrate a capability to learn.

Again, the hype picked up momentum to the extent that *The New York Times* reported that Rosenblatt had

> demonstrated the embryo of an electronic computer named the Perceptron which, when completed in about a year, is expected to be the first non-living mechanism able to, "perceive, recognize and identify its surroundings without human training or control." [And] that perceptrons would soon be able to beat humans at chess, identify images, and reproduce.[10]

However, the Mark I Perceptron faced significant limitations in, for instance, recognizing multiple types of patterns, which was one of the inefficiencies that Minsky and Papert had criticized in their book.

The term "AI winter" refers to a period when, after the euphoria of the initial advances of the AI programs, the overpromises for their impact are shown to be just that, overpromises. Then the pendulum swings against the optimists and stalls the process. Whereas funding was easily available during the good times, funding requests and, indeed, its spending, subsequently came under far greater scrutiny, which itself may be as unrealistically pessimistic as the euphoria was unrealistically optimistic. There are generally accepted to be two AI winters during the final three decades of the 20th century. Although there is agreement that there were two distinct periods, there are no specific dates. The first period loosely covered the 1970s and the second the 1990s with the 1980s somewhat of an AI spring.

To be fair, the overpromising (perhaps better expressed as overly optimistic predictions) prior to a winter was more likely to be the result of the natural exuberance that any researcher might experience when any sort of breakthrough is achieved. Even someone as eminent as Marvin Minsky was quoted as saying, in 1970, that "from three to eight years we will have a machine with the general intelligence of an average human being".[11] The AI research project led by Minsky and John McCarthy had received government funding of more than $2 million (equivalent to nearly $15 million in 2021 terms).

Similarly, throughout the 1960s, the Defense Advanced Research Projects Agency (DARPA) allocated significant funding in the millions of dollars with, it appears, no return on that investment even considered. The mantra seems to be – *here's some money, go away and spend it*. However, the lack of such financial performance metrics is arguably a necessity for conducting early research.

By the mid-1970s, it had become obvious that the earlier optimism was perhaps unrealistic, or at least premature. DARPA, for example, had become exasperated by the lack of progress on a *Speech Understanding Research* (SUR) program at Carnegie Mellon University, which was another contributor to the radical reduction in its funding for academic AI research.

On the other side of the Atlantic, also as a consequence of the unrealized optimism, the UK government commissioned a report on the potential for future AI development, which proved to be highly critical. Later known as the *Lighthill Report*,[12] it almost certainly led to the decision by the British government to end support for AI research in all but two universities. The Lighthill Report itself was later savaged by John McCarthy in a subsequent review.[13]

Irrespective of the merits of each position, this type of cycle in new technology is not unusual and may often simply be the consequence of bad luck. The Pony Express, for example, only lasted for about 18 months from opening to closing. It was put out of business by a thing called the telegraph arriving on the scene; microfiche was replaced by floppy disks, Blockbusters by streaming services and so on.

The speed of modern technological advances has made the acceptance of significant losses in the early stages of start-ups more common, with investors willing to bet on long-term returns. Companies such as Amazon, ESPN and Tesla all took between five and ten years (conservatively) to turn a profit. The strides made recently (detailed later in this book) and the funding attached to those strides may be a sign that AI has a robust future, especially in the sports industry.

NOTES

1. *50 People Who Fouled Up Football* by Michael Henderson (2009; Constable & Robinson).
2. Charles Reep (1904–2002): Pioneer of Notational and Performance Analysis in Football, *Journal of Sports Sciences*, 20, 2002, 853–5.
3. Ibid.
4. https://www.csail.mit.edu/about/mission-history
5. E. Cook, *Percentage Baseball*, MIT Press, Foreword, 1964.
6. Egor A. Timme, Alexander A. Dayal, and Yuri A. Kukushkin, *History of Cybernetics in Sports in the USSR Models Released in the 1960s*, 2020, History of Cybernetics in Sports in the USSR.pdf
7. S. Beer, *Brain of the Firm*, Wiley, 1972.
8. http://www.komkon.org/~ps/DK/zelen.html
9. Ibid.
10. *New York Times*, 13 July 1958.
11. Minsky has always argued that he was misquoted.

12. "Artificial Intelligence: A General Survey" by Professor Sir James Lighthill, FRS, in *Artificial Intelligence: A Paper Symposium*, Science Research Council 1973.

13. Review of "Artificial Intelligence: A General Survey" (The Lighthill Report) by John McCarthy, Computer Science Department, Stanford University, Stanford, CA.

3

SABERMETRICS, MONEYBALL AND AI

Sport tends to lag behind with the implementation of technological developments and so it was that, unfortunately, the *Society for American Baseball Research (SABR)* emerged just as AI as a discipline was entering its first winter in 1971. SABR was the idea of L. Robert (Bob) Davids, who brought together a group of fellow researchers at the National Baseball Hall of Fame in Cooperstown to establish the society. That inaugural meeting, which coincided with the 1971 Hall of Fame induction ceremony, was attended by what became known as the Cooperstown 16 – the founding fathers, so to speak.

In the intervening years, that number has grown to more than 5,000 with more than 20 different subgroups studying specific areas of the game, including what is now known as *Sabermetrics*, a term first coined by Bill James (who would become a champion for the study of baseball through statistics and analysis). In 1985, Bill James dedicated his landmark *Historical Baseball Abstract* to "the man who has done more for baseball research than anyone else living – L. Robert Davids".

The statistical analysis of baseball gradually spawned the use of similar methods in other sports. Bill James' real contribution was not necessarily in the quality of his analysis or, indeed, his statistical

DOI: 10.1201/9781003196532-5

expertise. It was more in how he developed his *Baseball Abstracts* style. Typically, James would begin his article with a question (e.g., "how valuable is the sacrifice bunt?"). He would then explain, through the presentation of detailed data, what he believed the answer to be and how he had arrived at that answer. Initially, James self-published his *Abstracts* because no major publisher understood that there would be a market for what they perceived as one man's musings. In reality, James would later come to be seen as the person who kick-started the analytics revolution across all sports.

Just as James was coining the term "sabermetrics", the first AI winter was ending, and the AI revolution was entering a relatively benign period during which another seminal work on sports analytics was produced. The writing team of John Thorn, Pete Palmer and David Reuther published *The Hidden Game of Baseball* in 1984. In Thorn's own words,

> The hidden game is the one played with statistics. It raises important questions about why we measure, what we think we are measuring, what we are truly measuring, and, most important, what the measurement means.[1]

As with Bill James, the real value of the book lay not with the purity or otherwise of the statistical analysis, but in interrogating and challenging the folklore that surrounds all sports, and all human endeavors, in fact. The authors moved the analysis from concern about RBI (runs batted in) totals, pitchers for wins and home run experts to metrics more focused on the central objective of the game – how to win. If the orthodoxies are challenged, analysis must follow and the analysis needs the data.

The 1980s was also somewhat of an AI spring in terms of funding. In its wisdom, the corporate world decided that investment in *expert systems*, programs that are designed to solve problems about a specific knowledge domain using the rules of logic, made sense. This method entails downloading the knowledge contained within the mind of a domain specialist and structuring that knowledge using a programmable set of rules. The Japanese government, for example, committed more than $2.5 billion (today's money) to a project to,

> write programs and build machines that could carry on conversations, translate languages, interpret pictures, and reason like human beings.[2]

At the same time, John Hopfield was creating his *Hopfield Networks* – a form of a *recurrent neural network* – that could learn and process information entirely differently from the earlier *Perceptrons*. Geoffrey Hinton and David Rumelhart were also working on what became known as the *backpropagation algorithm*. The *Hopfield Networks* and *Backpropagation* methods revived interest, and funding, in the field of artificial neural network research. Incidentally, when in 2019 Professor Hinton, the *Godfather of Deep Learning*, was awarded the Honda Prize,[3] the award citation stating that Hinton had "invented backpropagation" was criticized as inaccurate. Hinton acknowledged as much when he wrote that,

> I've seen things in the press that say that I invented backpropagation, and that is completely wrong. It's one of the rare cases where an academic feels he has got too much credit for something![4]

WINTER IS BACK BUT WE CAN STILL PLAY GAMES

As the 1980s decade neared its end, the first *World Congress of Science and Football* was established with the aim of connecting scientists, researchers and practitioners to disseminate knowledge on football analytics among other disciplines such as biomechanics, coaching, exercise physiology, performance profiling, psychology, sports medicine and training. Simultaneously, the cold winds of a second winter were felt when the market for specialized AI hardware, such as the LISP[5] machines, started to contract and eventually became irrelevant. If potential AI solutions to real-world challenges were proving elusive, it became questionable as to why specialist hardware would be needed to support such non-solutions.

It didn't help that, at the same time, IBM and Apple were producing desktops at far cheaper rates. LISP had become the Pony Express and the desktop PC was its telegraphic nemesis. While expert systems were still useful, they were only useful in a few specific contexts – not a good business model. By 1993, over 300 specialist AI companies had disappeared along with $1.5 billion (today's money) of turnover.

The winters, as in many hi-tech industries, suffered from the confluence of three simple issues: insufficient processing power to cope with the rapid advances in theory; a failure to deliver on promises to provide human-level intelligence; and the contraction of funding as a consequence of the first two problems exacerbating the slowdown. Again, as with many cycles, the winter was already beginning to thaw, and another spring was close at hand.

Notwithstanding the winter privations, there were continuing advances such as those made by IBM's Gerry Tesauro in developing TD-Gammon in 1992, a program which achieved human-level play in backgammon. This program represented an early demonstration of knowledge-free learning, which minimizes or, ideally, completely avoids the explicit integration of human expertise into the learning system. TD-Gammon achieves this through a combination of neural networks and "temporal difference learning", a technique that leverages differences in successive learner predictions to bootstrap and quickly learn from past knowledge, which has since proved effective for training expert-level policies in numerous games.

However, Tesauro was just one step in the march toward the primary goal of creating a genuine chess-playing machine. As far back as 1952, Arthur Samuel had effectively kick-started IBM's fascination with the role of games in solving the deeper problems of human intelligence when he developed the IBM 701, a very basic, yet very effective, checkers-playing program. His first learning program was completed in 1955.

Both were crucial steps toward chess-playing programs because they were early examples of using heuristic search methods. These methods use a so-called heuristic function assigning values to the different situations or "states" encountered in a game and played a key role in the later development of temporal-difference learning-based algorithms such as TD-Gammon.

After Tesauro's 1992 breakthrough with backgammon, it was the turn of chess to return to the front of the stage. In 1997, the victory of Deep Blue II, IBM's chess-playing program, over the incumbent world champion, Garry Kasparov, was the culmination of work that had started in earnest within IBM back in the 1980s. Work that had its origins in two programs, the ChipTest and Deep Thought, started at Carnegie Mellon University. In 1988, Deep Thought had become the first chess machine to beat a Grandmaster.

Later that same year, some of the Deep Thought team transferred to the IBM T.J. Watson Research Center to work on Deep Thought II which would morph into the first Deep Blue program. The first Deep Blue only played six games under tournament conditions, including losing to Garry Kasparov 4–2. After the Kasparov defeat, the team went back to the drawing board and resurfaced in May 1997 with Deep Blue II, beating Kasparov 3.5–2.5 (with two wins for Deep Blue II, one for Kasparov and the remainder draws).

Over 200 years since the Mechanical Turk fraudulently beat players around the globe, Deep Blue II had done so for real. Exactly 50 years before the Kasparov defeat, Norbert Wiener had written in what amounted to an afterthought in his book, Cybernetics, that,

> There is one question which properly belongs to this chapter [chapter eight], though it in no sense represents a culmination of its argument. It is the question whether it is possible to construct a chess-playing machine, and whether this sort of ability

represents an essential difference between the potentialities of the machine and the mind.

Wiener concluded that,

> Such a machine would not only play legal chess, but a chess not so manifestly bad as to be ridiculous. ... It would probably win over a stupid or careless chess player, and would almost certainly lose to a careful player of any considerable degree of proficiency. In other words, it might very well be as good a player as the vast majority of the human race. This does not mean that it would reach the degree of proficiency of Maelzel's fraudulent machine [von Kempelen's Turk], but for all that, it may attain a pretty fair level of accomplishment.[6]

Wiener may have underestimated the human ability to construct such a machine, but 50 years is a long time and human beings are incredible machines themselves. In the same year that Deep Blue beat Garry Kasparov, the first "RoboCup" match occurred, with the ultimate aim of creating a team of robots that can beat the human world champions in football by 2050. Incredible? Possibly.

THE MONEYBALL EFFECT

As TD-Gammon may have heralded the emergence from the second AI winter, the publication in 2003 of Moneyball: The Art of Winning an Unfair Game heralded the switch to a potentially glorious summer of statistics and AI for sports analytics. What Moneyball did was popularize the previously nerdy world of numbers. While neither the book nor the movie (2011) was about AI, rather they were about using data as a fundamental tool of problem-solving, it woke up the historically conservative confines of professional sport. It challenged the embedded myths of America's pastime through the use of data. The movie of the book, starring Brad Pitt, took the glamorization of sports analytics to another level.

The Moneyball "story" centers on Billy Beane, the General Manager of the Oakland Athletics baseball club. He manages to deliver a winning team (50%+) on a budget less than a third of those of the bigger teams such as the New York Yankees. He does so by using overlooked and undervalued statistical categories, such as on-base percentage, that baseball's good ol' boys willfully ignored, preferring to rely on their "gut". This enabled Beane to compete with the big boys while remaining within his lesser budget.

The movie appeared in the same year that IBM's Watson beat Jeopardy! champions Bradford Rutter and Ken Jennings. Four years later, DeepMind's AlphaGo beat European Go champion Fan Hui 5-0, going on a year later to beat arguably the world's best player, Lee Sedol, 4-1. AlphaGo's victory signified a major breakthrough for AI as the ancient game of Go had always been seen as the ultimate challenge for machines due to the intuitive and creative nature of the way the greatest human players play the game. In China, where the game has been played for millennia, it is perceived in almost spiritual terms as a metaphor for a connection with the soul of the universe – a connection that occurs through intuition, by "knowing without knowing how you know" – the type of statement often made by coaches to refute the need for stats and science.

Unlike Deep Blue, where human expert knowledge was meticulously embedded in the algorithm (ultimately involving over 8,000 handcrafted game features used to evaluate the machine's possible moves), AlphaGo was able to learn these features automatically by first examining data sets of human play, then using a technique known as deep reinforcement learning to iteratively improve its performance.

In deep reinforcement learning, humans simply provide the machine with goals, objectives and problems and then ask it to learn how best to achieve these goals through its own experiences and rewards (i.e., reinforcement) received from repeated interactions with the task at hand.

The machine achieves this through deep learning, typically using deep artificial neural networks, which implies the technique is "general-purpose" in that knowledge is not pre-codified (as with Deep

Blue); instead, the machines acquire knowledge by themselves, without relying on human expertise. Thus, *AlphaGo* was provided only with the rules of the game and by playing itself millions of times, learned and continued to learn as it progressed.

During the match against Lee Sedol, there were two magical moments in the five games. In Game Two, the machine made a move that, almost certainly, no human would contemplate or make – counter intuitive, therefore. The assembled expert audience audibly gasped and assumed that the machine had malfunctioned. It had not. *Move 37* may have been considered unimaginable in the thousands of years the game has been played. Surely, the day of the machine had come.

However, in Game Four, Lee Sedol responded with a move that defeated the machine by its human ingenuity. Sedol's *move 78* was a technical masterpiece that the machine may have not anticipated from the millions of games it played against itself during training, and ultimately considered extremely unlikely to happen in the real match-up. The reason this match and *moves 37* and *78* in themselves are so significant is that they jointly point to the growth of human learning through interaction with thinking machines. Humans and machines should be seen as cooperators, not competitors.

While *AlphaGo* learned its decision-making policies by first examining data sets of human expert play, the algorithm subsequently led to a generalized successor known as *AlphaZero*, earning its moniker from the fact that it requires zero examples of human expert behaviors. *AlphaZero* simply relied on knowledge of the rules of the game itself, which was demonstrated as it learned to play Go, Shogi and Chess at an expert level without any human supervision at all.

Yet, even successors have successors, and *AlphaZero* has itself been superseded by *MuZero*, which learns to master games without even knowing their rules ahead of time.

However, notwithstanding the intuitive nature of the top Go players, the game itself is still one of complete information – unlike sports. Would it be possible for an AI program to defeat players in games of incomplete information where bluffing (deception) can be a key factor in success? Could a machine in the 21st century prevail in von Neumann's challenge of playing poker at an advanced level? It turned out that the answer was "yes!"

As the 2010s passed their midpoint, *DeepStack* became the first computer program to beat professional players at "heads-up, no-limit Hold 'em Poker" in 2016. The next target was to beat numerous poker players in a multi-player game. The problem with a heads-up game is that with only two players, there is only one hand to beat. With a multi-handed game, there are naturally four or five players who may have a better hand than the bot, not only a better hand but also a great hand that is unlikely to be bluffed. With that in mind, the opportunities to bluff recede and the complexity of decision-making increases.

On the heels of *DeepStack* came the work of the Carnegie Mellon team led by Tuomas Sandholm and Noam Brown. They were jointly responsible for three poker-playing programs – *Claudico*, *Libratus* and *Pluribus*.

The first two were limited to one versus one heads-up situations, but the third, *Pluribus*, achieved the breakthrough of winning in a multi-player situation. Pluribus was conservative in its methodology, relying on creating copies of itself, which then played against themselves to create a strategic template of how to play the game. What made the difference was the scale. The program could repeatedly play against itself millions of times and remember which strategies worked best. In doing so it effectively replicated and simultaneously enhanced the heuristically based human learning process.

Having learned the best strategies by playing against itself, *Pluribus* then played 10,000 games against five human players, plus a further 10,000 involving five *Pluribus* bots played against one professional poker player. *Pluribus* came out on top in both challenges.

While machine intelligence was exhibiting technical prowess against humans in poker, another competition was evolving between human-designed machines and machines driven by humans (bots vs. Esports champions). In 2019, after two previous failed attempts, *OpenAI Five* (OpenAI's autonomous bot) overcame a four-time Dota

Major Championship winning team. OpenAI managed to win 99.4% of the more than 7,000 games it played, with many of those victories coming from some of the nearly 700 games it played against 1,500+ players simultaneously.[7]

In the last two years of the decade, *AlphaStar*, DeepMind's *StarCraft II* playing program, comprehensively beat a top professional player, Team Liquid's Grzegorz "MaNa" Komincz. This was significant because AI had, until that time, struggled to tame the complexity of StarCraft. Real-Time Strategy (RTS) games, and StarCraft, in particular, have been viewed as one of the most significant challenges that AI needed to surmount. It is also one of the most significant for the future of AI in sport – the ultimate real-time strategy environment.

The 2010s have seen an acceleration in the advances made by the AI community, possibly greater than at any time in the past. Although it may have taken thousands of years to reach the technological advances of today, another AI winter of the same scale as those in past eras seems less and less likely to occur, and almost impossible to imagine in the near future for sport, where the value of cognitive diversity and technological enhancement seem finally to have become accepted.

The utility of games in the development of AI has been essential to its development; it is now time for AI to return the favor and enhance the development of sport. The next part of the book will outline where the relationship between sport and AI currently stands.

NOTES

1. *The Hidden Game of Baseball*, 2015 by John Thorn, Our Game (mlblogs.com).
2. Pamela McCorduck, *Machines Who Think* (2nd ed.), Natick, MA: A. K. Peters, Ltd., 2004.
3. The Honda Prize is awarded annually in recognition of the work of individuals or groups generating new knowledge to drive the next generation of AI from the standpoint of eco-technology.

4. https://medium.com/syncedreview/who-invented-backpropagation-hinton-says-he-didnt-but-his-work-made-it-popular-e0854504d6d1

5. LISP is one of the oldest of the families of programming languages.

6. N. Wiener, *Cybernetics*, Wiley, 1947, p. 192/3 NOTE.

7. https://www.joindota.com/news/81450-openai-defeats-99-4-of-human-players-over-the-weekend#comment:5349753

Part 2

WHERE ARE WE NOW?

4

TECHNOLOGY CLOSES
THE GAP ON THEORY

It's early morning at an elite football club and the staff are beginning to set things up prior to the arrival of the players. Such staff might typically include the coaches, chefs, kit handlers, masseurs, strength conditioners, fitness trainers, medical teams and now, more and more commonly in the modern game, a team of data analysts with an understanding of the value of artificial intelligence (AI) to the ultimate success of the club's various efforts. And, the same scene will be played out at every other center of sporting excellence in every other sport, be it team sports, individual sports or a combination of both, such as with elite cycling.

Just as the theory of marginal gains,[1] consistently cited as key to the success of British Cycling under Dave Brailsford, became an accepted (and also well critiqued) model, it was, in the manner of innovations, copied and implemented by others, thus closing the competitive gap. So too, the need to close competitive gaps ensures that AI will become increasingly important in identifying and taking advantage of gains, marginal or otherwise, across the entire sporting ecosystem – an ecosystem that incorporates all elements indicated in Figure 4.1, either around the game or in the game.

Technology and processing power are no longer the inhibitors to the advance of AI in sport that they once were. In F1, for example,

DOI: 10.1201/9781003196532-7

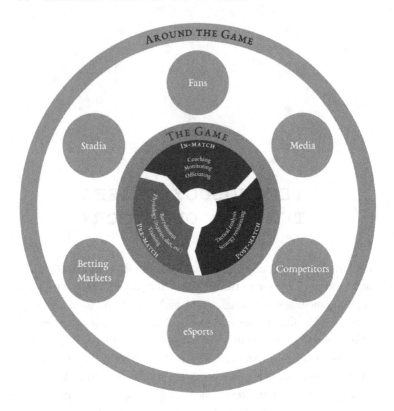

Figure 4.1 The sporting ecosystem

everything from the driver to the car itself can be measured to the nth degree and aggregated to deliver advantages of 1000th of a second that can decide the race. The vehicles themselves have as many as 400 sensors and the drivers are connected to biometric and other health-related data collectors. As if to make the point that the central theme of AI is the interrelationship between humans and machines and the enhancement of that relationship, the role of AI in sport is balanced between the health of the technology and the health of the athletes. AI is now a central component of the medical well-being of athletes.

AI can provide a comparative analysis on a variety of health parameters, which can themselves be provided by AI-supported wearable technology. AI helps in streaming and collating the health-related data and avoiding major health-related problems later. All of this type of information, now amounting to more than 60 years' worth in F1, is stored in the cloud and available for analysis to the management team that may be thousands of miles away, but crucially contributing to making real-time decisions at the track.

Nevertheless, a race can also be decided by a mistimed overtaking procedure – a driver error due to their interaction with a car they are physically situated within. We could, of course, eliminate the physical car altogether, but where's the fun in that? Apparently, there is great fun in that, as the phenomenon of Esports is demonstrating. In fact, that may well be precisely where we are headed. Notwithstanding the ultimate destination for sports, currently it is the interaction between humans and machines that provides the fascination for the fans. There are also opportunities like fans being able to digitally interact with an F1 team in real time, for example, that will add a further level of connection for the fan experience. All of this will increasingly be aided by AI in one form or another.

As with all innovations, there are advocates and naysayers to such developments. At the time of writing, it seems that the advocates may have the edge and that we are standing at the entrance to exciting breakthroughs in the interaction between machines and humans in the world of sporting endeavors. This part of the book will examine the claims and counterclaims as to just where AI and sport actually stand at the start of the 2020s.

THEORETICAL ALTERNATIVES

The evolution of AI may have arrived at a place where the battleground between contesting approaches has tilted in favor of what are sometimes referred to as the "connectionists" over the early leaders, the "symbolists".[2] The "connectionists" believe that at some stage in the future, however long that might be, computers will be able to genuinely mimic the way in which humans learn. This model posits that the way ahead is by "training" the machine to engage in billions of trials against an ideal outcome to inexorably narrow in on the solution. Conversely, the "symbolists" reject that vision of the future in favor of the notion that machines can only operate by following discrete (logic-based) rules. The machine's instructions are contained in specific symbols and that is a uniquely mechanistic way of learning.

Following a more "connectionist" definition, AI can be simplified as those programs that are able to demonstrate the ability to learn and to reason in a manner indistinguishable from humans. The subcategories of such programs (see Figure 4.2) would be "machine learning" (ML), which consists of specific algorithms designed to learn without being explicitly programmed, and a further subset of ML itself, "deep learning" (DL), which is a class of machine learning techniques that use multilevel hierarchies (i.e., layers) of increasingly abstract representations to learn concepts and make decisions given rich inputs (e.g., as images, videos, audio waveforms or combinations thereof).

As the onion layers of AI are peeled back, ever further layers are revealed. ML, for example, is traditionally broken into three further subfields – "supervised learning", "unsupervised learning" and "reinforcement learning".

In *supervised learning*, the task is for the program to learn a model that, given specific inputs, is able to predict specific outputs.

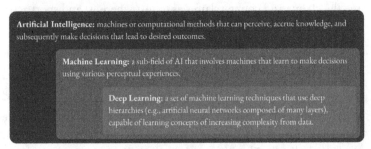

Figure 4.2 AI subcategories

The term "supervised" refers to the fact that the datasets such as techniques used for training specify both the inputs used to make decisions and the corresponding outputs expected; i.e., the machine receives a *supervisory* signal that maps all inputs to corresponding outputs. In supervised "classification", these outputs are referred to as labels, for example, labels tagging various categories of events to time frames of broadcast video of a football match (e.g., "was the event that occurred at this moment in the video a pass, a shot or a clearance?"). Supervised "regression" does not target a categorical label but rather predicts a numerical quantity (e.g., the numerical probability of a player action resulting in a goal-scoring event).

With *unsupervised learning*, the task is to understand patterns in the space of the data itself, with no concrete input–output pairs (or "labels") in the training dataset. The machine is learning without a supervisor just as humans do most of the time. In this learning regime, relationships between the raw data points themselves are automatically discovered to better understand the domain at hand (e.g., positive or negative correlations between certain events, clusters or patterns that exist in the data). An example would be to cluster attributes of football players (e.g., their on-pitch behaviors such as locations where they take shots, pass and make intercepts, and physical characteristics such as heights and ages) to identify players of similar characteristics (e.g., for scouting purposes).

Reinforcement learning entails a learning agent, an entity capable of receiving sensory observations as inputs and delivering decisions as outputs, which enables it to achieve certain goals. Agents are typically goal-oriented and show proactive behavior in interacting within an environment to then receive feedback in the form of rewards (or costs), ideally learning decision-making policies that maximize their cumulative rewards. As such, reinforcement learning is often considered to be situated between the extremes of supervised and unsupervised learning, in the sense that there are no labeled examples available as in unsupervised learning, but there is a feedback signal in the form of reward that tells an agent how desirable the actions are that it is taking. Reinforcement learning, for example, can be used to train robotic agents that physically play football, with "goals scored" being the obvious rewards in such a scenario.

A large part of human-centric sports analytics leverages supervised and unsupervised learning (as they primarily result in models that can be used for predictions or understanding of games). On the other hand, reinforcement learning is foreseen as being increasingly useful for designing tactical strategies for players to maximize long-term rewards. Specifically, one may consider an entire football match as a sequential decision-making problem involving multiple interacting agents (human decision-makers in this case) that seek to maximize their rewards. Under such a view of a match and with corresponding models for the player dynamics/interactions involved, reinforcement learning algorithms can be deployed that seek to learn policies mapping a given in-game situation to a corresponding set of actions or tactical suggestions for the players.

Such a sequential decision-making view can then be abstracted even further under the reinforcement learning paradigm, for instance, by considering not just the players' actions taken in a single match-up, but a sequence of match-ups within a league, each rewarding the team if their sequence of decisions leads them to a victory, and penalizing the team for each loss.

As Figure 4.1 highlights, the effect of AI on the sporting environment is all-pervasive. Within the competitive arenas themselves, AI is, or should be, intimately involved before, during and after the games. In reality, the same should be true of the situations around the game. The purpose of any AI intervention is to increase performance levels, understanding of the game and the overall human experience of the sport and should, therefore, be judged on those metrics.

NOTES

1. The theory of marginal gains basically argues that if the team were to break down every component of their performance and subsequently improve each component by 1%, it should automatically achieve a significant aggregated increase in performance.

2. This "battle" is well covered in Cade Metz's book, *Genius Makers: The Mavericks Who Brought AI to Google, Facebook and the World* (Random House Business), 2021. Metz is currently lead writer on technology issues for the *New York Times*.

5

THE SPORTS ECOSYSTEM

FEEDBACK LOOPS

The feedback loops that surround the games themselves are vitally important to the ultimate performance delivered on match day by everyone involved at each level. Preparation for any game is informed by feeding back post-game tactical analysis and biometric and recovery data, a task almost created for AI assistance. Before the whistle blows to start any game is a period wherein the health of the players can be monitored, and interventions proposed and enacted, a period in which tactics can be designed before they are enacted and then assessed for their effectiveness. During the game, biometric and performance data can be fed instantaneously to management and coaching staff and then to the players. After each match, post-game analysis takes place and is used to prepare for the next games and so the cycle becomes one of continuous learning and implementation with AI involved at every stage.

However, the other key feedback loop is that which takes place within the talent cycle system. As Figure 5.1 indicates, this process has distinct stages that are in perpetual movement clockwise around the cycle, with each stage constantly interacting with its two adjacent neighbors. Each of the stages is inevitable and has to be managed, and AI can support each of them.

DOI: 10.1201/9781003196532-8

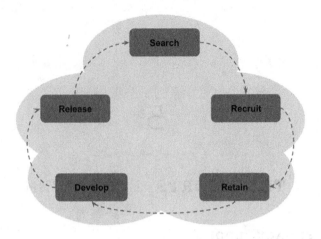

Figure 5.1 Feedback stages

Probably the best place to locate the analysis loop that represents the talent management within a club is with the identification, recruitment, retention, development and ultimately the exit of players and staff. The early identification of talent can be worth millions of dollars in terms of player acquisition, development and subsequent trading for team sports. In individual sports such as tennis and golf, being identified by managers/agents can provide early financial support for the players that in itself can contribute to ultimate success. Identifying young tennis players or golfers can provide considerable commercial returns as can the development and trading of players in team sports. In elite football, for example, player trading has become a recognized fourth revenue stream in addition to the traditional three streams of match day, commercial and broadcasting.

Recruitment and scouting provide opportunities where AI and Big Data have already had a significant effect. Currently, scouting tends to use traditional approaches, albeit significantly enhanced by modern technological advances. Analyzing video imagery and the CGI (Computer Generated Imagery) derived from those images has been a mainstay of recruitment analytics for some time. A plethora of companies have been delivering analytical tools for the use of elite football clubs in the top European leagues for some time now.

The tools they provide can also be used by agents, coaches and individual players themselves. They enable the clubs to outsource what can be a resource-intensive activity. While scouting talent has moved on from the team of roaming human scouts only able to see a finite number of players in a finite number of games into a much greater reliance on technology, the process still requires a large and often laborious human input. This is where AI is beginning to make its contribution.

AI can replace the need for a human being to wade through mountains of data extracted from video coverages delivered by a variety of TV and streaming organizations as well as wearable tech, drone technology and static audiovisual instrumentation within stadiums. All of that data can then be analyzed by AI, for example, both to better understand the coordination between players on the team and to conceptualize an ideal profile for the type of player required to fill a particular role within the tactical configuration of the team.

This profile can also be used to provide the template against which potential recruitment targets might be assessed. Machine learning enables the template to be continuously updated and improved such that the talent identification process itself is continuous.

Another way in which the traditional methods of recruitment can be streamlined is through the use of AI-assisted virtual reality software. Game-specific skills can be built into drills that can be measured by AI technology in quick time and immediately compared to the metrics of top players at similar stages of their development. As an aid to progressing or rejecting a high volume of "walk-on" players, it could prove invaluable by increasing the size of the entry end of the talent funnel.

More advanced skills such as the scanning abilities of top players in team sports can be assessed as part of early talent ID, particularly for certain functions in football. Scanning is perhaps most easily described as the ability of players to visualize their surroundings when in play, thus enabling them to make better decisions. Imagine the awareness that the ever-alert meerkats appear to demonstrate, a sort of constant surveillance of their immediate environment. Players such as Pirlo, Xavi and Zidane (readers use your own list) are known to make significantly greater head and body movements in the ten seconds prior to receiving a pass than the average player. Using such data can also be used as a benchmark for coaching youth players and aid the development stage of the cycle.

Unfortunately, technology is still an inhibiting factor in this particular topic. As Kredel et al. point out in their impressive meta-study of the more than 60 studies on "gaze behavior" in sports using eye-tracking technology over the past 45 years,

> in order to increase the amounts of data acquired for the derivation of reliable results, the development of high-frequent and robust eye-trackers, integrated in positioning systems to allow for the algorithmic gaze-cue allocation of large amounts of raw gaze data, stands as the major challenge of sport science.[1]

As the quality of AI-supported technology advances, this may become one of the key areas of research for all sports in the not-too-distant future.

On a more commercial note, the data from senior players can be used in transfer dealings, and using virtual reality headsets as an alternative to players standing around in inclement weather can be a more effective use of coaching time and space. The gamification[2] of the data for learning-facilitation (currently only delivered in the pre-season play book tomes so beloved of NFL coaches) can actually be delivered through apps that players can use when injured or in pre-season, and are known to enhance learning performance.

R.C. Buford (GM of the San Antonio Spurs) describes an AI-enhanced decision-making process as one that

> seeks alignment of the multi-variables – the eyes (scouting), the ears (intelligence), the numbers (performance). If we're going to deviate from what the eyes, ears, and numbers are telling us then there needs to be a really good reason. We would need to dig much deeper. ... When the alignment between the eyes,

ears and numbers isn't there, falling back on the process and the
data allows you to ask better questions.[3]

Those sentiments signal the way ahead as being a symbiotic learning
relationship between the numbers and intuition, between humans
and machines. In sport, the type of measurement that adds value
to the coaching and medical staff is of such complexity and infini-
tesimal detail that humans need help, and AI can provide that help.
As Roberto Martinez, the Belgium National Team Manager and
Technical Director of the Belgian FA, believes,

> It's essential, for an analyst, for a coach, for a team, for a player,
> to access the latest technology. It allows you to be at the fore-
> front of being part of a high-performance environment.[4]

The involvement of AI at each stage of the talent cycle will provide a
significant competitive advantage.

STAYING HEALTHY

Irrespective of how talented athletes are, they cannot perform if they
are not healthy, both physically and mentally. Given the increasing
granularity of health and safety data (and especially individualized
data), AI/ML can now be applied to tasks well beyond game day
performance, for the benefit of players and, indeed, of coaches. In
fact, in terms of cardiac problems, coaches appear to be particularly vulnerable. In football, for example, Jock Stein died in the dugout, Johan Cruyff, Ronald Koeman, Graeme Souness and Gerrard
Houllier suffered serious heart attacks, as did others in US sports
such as the Chicago Bears' Mike Ditka, Bill Parcells who required
surgery in 1992, Dennis Green of the Minnesota Vikings and Arizona
Cardinals, who died during a cardiac arrest in 2016. Tony Sparano
of the Miami Dolphins and Oakland Raiders died of heart disease
in 2018. Bruce Arians then of the Arizona Cardinals, Todd Bowles,
ex-NY Jets, and Mike Zimmer of the Minnesota Vikings also made
trips to emergency rooms.

The job of head coach is considered one of the most important to the success of major sporting franchises, and one of the highest paid. As such, these employees are human assets that require constant attention. Their working schedules are incredibly stressful and their personal health regimes generally appalling – poor diet, 80 hours plus working weeks, high travel mileage, results-driven and normally highly driven personalities.

Of course, it is not only in the dugout that such health issues occur as the Christian Eriksen on-field health incident at Euro 2020 reminded us. The sports authorities will probably have to accept that wearable AI technology may have to be permitted in the future. It would have the benefit of protecting the player and providing a range of biometrical and health data in real time, with the usual caveats regarding logistical, privacy and regulatory issues.

Finally, such personalities are generally reluctant to proactively subject themselves to regular health checks. AI-supported wearable technology can take on that role for them. And the data from wearable tech could be transported to the athletes'/coaches' employers without any physical intrusion subject, of course, to the prevailing confidentiality regulations. AI/ML can immediately begin to learn about such key patterns/trends in metrics such as heart rate variability (HRV), which current research suggests is a key indicator of real and potential health issues in elite athletes. The business models of wearable technology companies such as *WHOOP* or *FitBit* are based on using the high-performance needs of elite athletes to sell their products to the mass markets represented by the average person's desire to stay healthy.

INJURIES AND WELL-BEING

Of a lower order of concern than life-threatening health issues, yet quite crucial in the sporting context, is the ability to predict and prevent injury, and should that fail, to aid the speediest recovery. Real-time monitoring of training workloads using wearable tech, for example, has been able to predict injuries to elite footballers within a week prior to matches by combining such data with an accuracy close to 90%.

In football, the current programs are most accurate at predicting the risk of ankle and hamstring injuries and reasonably accurate with knee and other lower leg injuries. Such examples have been found to be responsible for more than 60% of all injury-related absences. In basketball, another high-intensity sport where repetitive actions such as jumping (and high-impact landing) are exacerbated by changing direction, knee (ligament- and patellar-related) and Achilles injuries are commonplace. In such scenarios, AI could analyze and enable the development of strategies to reduce the occurrences and severity of injuries.

AI can also help to make the increasing use of concussion protocols more efficient. Early research into the prevalence of chronic traumatic brain injury among retired professional boxers found that approximately 17% exhibited recognizable characteristics.[5] More recently, in the United States, Dr. Bennet Omalu, a forensic pathologist, became the first to publish evidence of chronic traumatic encephalopathy (CTE) in retired NFL players.[6] Further evidence has emerged from other studies of CTE in both American football and ice hockey players, some of which show that more than 80% of a control group of 200+ NFL players were found to be affected by CTE.[7] Nearly all of those 80%+ with CTE symptoms, irrespective of the severity, had cognitive symptoms and mood disorders and signs of dementia.

Evidence is also growing of similar concerns in football (soccer) and rugby players. The type of accurate and speedy monitoring enabled by AI can help elite sports organizations and individual athletes to provide early diagnosis and treatment for any identified neuro-anomalies before the situation becomes irretrievable.

In terms of efficiency, AI enables the limited amount of monitoring that individual humans are able to conduct to be expanded exponentially. Metrics such as high-intensity interval training (HIIT), running, acute and chronic training load figures, distance covered at various speeds, accelerations and decelerations, sleep quality, HRV trends and recent injury history can all be fed into a single AI/ML program and can provide de-risking recommendations based on the learning delivered by the program itself. As the program continues to learn in real time, it can transmit that learning to its human partners and provide those partners with detailed and, more importantly, continuous real-time information. In that way, knowledge of physical well-being and learning does not stagnate.

NOTES

1. *Front. Psychol.*, 17 October 2017 | https://doi.org/10.3389/fpsyg.2017. 01845, *Eye-Tracking Technology and the Dynamics of Natural Gaze Behavior in Sports: A Systematic Review of 40 Years of Research* by Ralf Kredel, Christian Vater, André Klostermann and Ernst-Joachim Hossner, University of Bern, Bern, Switzerland.

2. *A Generalized Method for Empirical Game Theoretic Analysis.* Karl Tuyls, Julien Perolat, Marc Lanctot, Joel Z. Leibo, Thore Graepel. AAMAS 2018.

3. Interview with authors, March 2021.

4. Interview with authors.

5. M.H. Rabadi and B.D. Jordan, "The Cumulative Effect of Repetitive Concussion in Sports", *Clinical Journal of Sport Medicine*, 11, 3, 2001 July, 194–198.

6. Dr Omalu's research was popularized in the 2015 movie, *Concussion*, starring Will Smith.

7. Orit H. Lesman-Segev, Lauren Edwards, Gil D. Rabinovicl, *Chronic Traumatic Encephalopathy: A Comparison with Alzheimer's Disease and Frontotemporal Dementia.*

6

THE PERFORMANCE

PREPARATION

Until recent years, sports analysts have typically used what are now seen as rudimentary statistical methods primarily to process strongly labeled data (e.g., aggregation statistics computed using event stream data, or simple models using tracking data). These data types are traditionally difficult to obtain (requiring either human annotators or specialized hardware installed on a case-by-case basis in stadiums or training venues). However, technological developments are now occurring which enable data to be automatically generated directly from video imagery, thus removing humans-in-the-loop and automatically producing as human-interpretable performance statistics.

As such, AI is increasingly able to provide greater assistance to the coaching community and, through the consequent coaching activity, affect the ultimate performance of the athletes themselves whether they are competing in teams or individually. In baseball, for example, recruitment and line-up decisions are increasingly influenced by machine learning capabilities unimaginable to Billy Beane and his revolutionaries of more than 20 years ago.

On the mound, the exact trajectory of a curve ball or the variability of a knuckleball can be assessed to millimeters. Similarly, in tennis, it is now possible to measure the speed and spin of a ball off the racket. In football, ball spin and flight patterns can be tracked so

DOI: 10.1201/9781003196532-9

that the precise amount of bend delivered by modern Beckhams can be accurately measured. In fact, it is becoming possible to measure almost anything, which increases the possibilities for the machines to create continuous learning cycles.

As part of the 2020 Olympics in Tokyo, Alibaba/Intel's jointly developed 3D Athlete Tracking application will be used to create 3D representations of athletes in action from which coaches can extract real-time data. *Alibaba* and *Intel* provide the two vital components – video quality and processing power – to create the final product, which is a digital model of the performance. The video images are transformed by the AI algorithm to create a product that can be analyzed either at leisure or in real time to compare an athlete's performance against themselves or their competitors or even against an AI-generated "ideal" competitor.

SPACE – THE FINAL FRONTIER

Another significant development, in team sports especially, is the increased understanding of the use of space that machine learning can provide. The use of SNA (Social Network Analysis) modeling of behavioral patterns during in-game action has been enabled by the processing and learning capacity provided by AI.[1] One aspect of this is the work being done using deep learning to predict future movements (trajectories) of players so that the movements of both teammates and opponents can be anticipated.

Such systems learn by tracking player and ball movements at high frequency (e.g., 25 frames-per-second) throughout all matches, comprising millions of data points in total. Other variables, such as the role of each player (as designated by the coaches), can be added to increase the potential learning opportunities for the machine. By utilizing what are referred to as predictive modeling techniques, it becomes possible to create entire hypothetical or scenario planning-generated games which can then be played out by the machines.[2]

Predictive models can show in-play movement simultaneously with the live play, represented by animated dots on a graphic representation of the pitch. In addition, providing tracking data for each team, so-called ghosting techniques, enables a third defensive team to be simulated, representing how the *average or best/worst* teams in any league would defend a similar situation.

Stats Perform, a major player in this sector, is also working with coaches to provide interactive simulations using real-time play sketching.

> A coach can draw out a play that they want their players to perform on their clipboard and what tracking data and technology can do is to make intelligent clipboards that can simulate how that play drawn by the coach would play out.[3]

The potential for collaboration with Esports expertise could further increase the learning from which coaches would benefit.

It becomes possible to develop tactics for set plays (for and against) and to test those tactics against other machines in much the same way that *AlphaGo* learned to outperform the top human players. Gamifying the results of tactical schemes could also be provided on Apps for players to develop their personal learning of game management, for example, during down times, such as when injured or suspended.

Notwithstanding the tactical advantage that AI can provide prior to the game, it can also deliver real-time in-game analysis for the coaches. It can quantify an individual athlete's physical strain parameters to predict endurance degradation throughout matches. For five-set matches at grand slam tennis tournaments, for example, such data would be a key competitive advantage. Ultimately, it will be for the player and coach to decide on the detailed tactics for specific matches, but the information provided by AI could be the decisive factor.

CONTINUOUS LEARNING

A combination of sensor technology and AI can also help coaches improve players' techniques. For example, in weight training — now almost universal across sports — AI can provide instantaneous feedback to maximize the results of a workout and create personalized training programs.

The training and coaching of athletes and, indeed, of the coaches and managers themselves should be a continuous learning process that also needs to be able to prioritize learning from and for specific events. Arguably, the pedagogical application of machine learning (i.e., "machine teaching", or more accurately, "facilitated learning") has been underexplored in the past and yet has huge potential for aiding human decision-making, whether in sport or otherwise.

The sports industry, however, has woken up to this potential and has already deployed a number of techniques for assisting coaches to not just understand what to teach, but how to teach/train players based on specific in-match situations. One spin-off from the AI-driven coaching approaches for elite athletes is that the resultant output can be made as accessible to amateur athletes and coaches as they are to elite athletes and coaches.

THE ELITES

For AI systems to challenge the conventional notions of coaching excellence, they need to improve the results and simultaneously reduce the workload needed to administer the process. In the early days of "AI coaching", the former was only possible with what seemed to many to be an actual *increase* in human workload. The AI of those early days did little more than describe certain elements of the performance and as each new element was considered, it would lead to more and more coding work for the back office.

Similarly, while trying to predict (e.g., injuries) adds greater value to the results, the workload on humans also increases significantly. Also, most of the earlier systems would only predict potentially "negative" consequences such as intensity overload while still being unable to propose "positive" plans such as an optimal real-time agenda for that day's/week's program. And this is where "reinforcement learning" (RL) enters the conversation by removing the need for resource-intensive human involvement.

With RL, the coach/manager provides the machine with a clear objective, to achieve an optimal level of fitness, for example, while avoiding serious injury or risking future availability for the match days. From that moment, the machine does its thing – it learns through processing millions of simulations (learning events). As it learns, it refines and narrows into the final proposal. It then delivers that proposal to the coaching staff and they decide on the applicability of the proposal. In the words of Thierry Geerts, "the machine proposes, the human decides".[4]

The National Football League (NFL) in the United States is a fertile ground for deep learning research and its stop/start discrete play structure makes experimentation and analysis easier than with association football (soccer). For example, current programs can predict the expected yardage from running plays by providing data from a runner's teammates, opponents, the handoff and first contact. As such, the AI coach can provide the human coach with the probabilities of success for any proposed play.

THE AMATEURS

All sports are now selling off-the-peg versions of bespoke AI technology initially developed for the elite market. During the Covid-19 pandemic, such wearable or home-based technology grew in popularity primarily because it enabled people to continue to connect with other exercisers in a more socially and epidemiologically acceptable way. Wearable technology companies have seen a rise in the volume of recorded activity on their apps, and those who already had the apps seem to be increasing their own workouts by more than 10%.[5]

Other technologies, such as the iPhone *HomeCourt* basketball app, enable the user to capture data on "events" such as shooting through the phone's camera. Such apps also enable individuals to benchmark themselves against NBA professionals who have provided similar data. All of the data can then be reused for whatever purpose HomeCourt wishes. In a similar vein *PerfectPlay*, an app designed in collaboration with the 2021 Champions' League winners, Chelsea FC, provides a related service to the football community.

Typical professional training games have been digitized in a program combining computer vision and advanced machine learning capabilities which, according to the developers,

> allows us to perceive comprehensive human-centered scenes and grasps their physical, cognitive, and emotional aspects. By combining those capabilities with professional knowledge of teachers, it allows building AI teachers that analyze students and provide personalized feedback on how to improve in real-time.[6]

Grandiose claims, perhaps, but a clear ambition of any AI program.

Although such developments are meant for non-elite athletes, the commercial rewards are by no means amateurish. In 2020, for example, Mustard, a company using a motion analysis app for generic athletics coaching, managed to raise $1.7 million in funding from serious investment companies as well as ex-major league players such as Drew Brees (top NFL QB) and Nolan Ryan (MLB Hall of Famer). The business model is to make elite coaching available to all athletes, although, as the investment group shows, the initial focus will be on baseball with the app providing pitchers of any standard personalized online instruction based on data extracted from huge biometrics databases. The app uses a combination of algorithms and a computer vision system which uses routine video technology to capture imagery from the user's mobile phone to evaluate the individual's game-related biomechanics.

NOTES

1. See, for example, "Defining a historic football team: using Network Science to analyze Guardiola's F.C. Barcelona" by J.M. Buldú, J. Busquets, I. Echegoyen and F. Seirul.lo, in *Scientific Reports*, volume 9, Article number: 13602, 2019.
2. This topic is available in detail at https://jair.org/index.php/jair/article/view/12505

3. Artificial Intelligence (AI) in Sports, *Sport Performance Analysis*.

4. Comment by Geerts in meetings with the authors. For more details, see *Homo Digitalis: Hoe digitalisering ons meer mens maakt* (Dutch Edition) by Geerts, Thierry; Translated in English: *How digitization makes us more human*.

5. https://www.sciencedirect.com/science/article/pii/S1389128620 1001651

6. https://www.calcalistech.com/ctech/articles/0,7340,L-3844814,00. html

7

AI IN THE GAME

As much as the role of AI in *preparing* to play any sport is important, a large part of the current interest in AI is due to the role that AI plays in what happens on the field/court/track *during* the games. The increase in the possibilities of AI in sports has been driven by the rapid advances in algorithmic capacity, increasing computational capacity and the exponential growth in data capacity (Big Data). Data especially plays a key role in breathing new life into relatively stagnant fields. In sports analytics, for example, there has been a proliferation in companies specializing in data collection and categorization.

Traditional forms of data exist on a spectrum of granularity and information content from the least to most granular. For example, the data types in football range from event stream data, summarizing all on-the-ball events (e.g., passes, shots) in a game; tracking data, capturing the 3D positions of all players and the ball at high frame rates; broadcast or tactical video footage capturing the state of players (and additional information such as body orientations, joint angles, etc.) throughout the match.

All sports now routinely use machine learning to greater or lesser degrees. As mentioned previously, in basketball, combining computer vision with machine learning provides accurate metrics for such elements as shot accuracy, speed across the court, vertical jump, speed of ball release and other ball-handling skills. Additionally, it

DOI: 10.1201/9781003196532-10

enables coaches to view 3D representations of biomechanical data while minimizing the need for sensors and/or body suits attached to the athletes. In cricket, not only can the speed of the ball through the air be measured, but also its speed upon impact, its position on the bat, the torque on impact and the effectiveness of the resultant shot.

Such "event stream data" with its associated annotated time-stamps of key on-the-ball events adds to the knowledge base for all coaches – if they can interpret it and then apply it. Similarly, "tracking data" using high-speed recording technology can provide XYZ positions of all players and the ball. A relatively recent addition to the football statistics tool kit is what researchers from KU Leuven and data intelligence company *SciSports* (Enschede, the Netherlands) call VAEP (Valuing Actions by Estimating Probabilities). The concept attempts to link how players' actions affect the result of a game by analyzing both offensive and defensive contributions. The model does this by evaluating the effect of each and every on-the-ball action – shots, passes, dribbles, tackles, etc. – of which there can be as many as 2000 per game, on the result.

The authors argue that by using this evaluation system, talent acquisition in the elite leagues can benefit by uncovering value similar to the original *Moneyball* model. An example quoted in the article was that while Marcus Rashford and Ousmane Dembélé were the two top-rated players in 2019,

> the fourth-ranked but lesser known Jonjoe Kenny had a much lower estimated market value than both of these players due to two reasons. First, Kenny is a defensive player, who are typically valued lower than offensive players by clubs and fans. Second, Kenny plays for mid-table club Everton, where he is surrounded by only a few world-class players. Nevertheless, our player ratings suggest a much higher valuation than his current estimated market value of € 5 million.[1]

For *SciSports*, therefore, Kenny represented greater value than either Rashford or Dembélé. Unfortunately, the market has its own logic and Kenny was sold for his estimated value of €5 million. Notwithstanding, the model does have value and is only possible as a result of the growing capabilities that the combination of machine learning and data availability provide.

Other recent advances include contextualized event stream data (a combination of event stream and partial tracking data). AI programs can fully or semi-autonomously learn from huge, complicated data-sets enabling classification, reinforcement learning, pattern identification and network analysis. However, such programs are not without shortcomings. For example, as VAEP demonstrates in football, it is extremely difficult to fully contextualize the almost infinite situations in which actions are performed and therefore to ascribe value to those actions. Also, notwithstanding the predictive modeling and network analysis approaches mentioned earlier, it remains very difficult to measure the value and use of space and more significantly deceptive practices such as reverse passing, decoy running and deceptive eye movements.

An Off-the-Ball Scoring Opportunity (OBSO) model addresses one of the "unseen" events that rarely gets attention in football, that is the quality of players' positioning to receive a pass in high-opportunity scoring positions. This enables players to receive credit for being in the right place at the right time irrespective of the arrival of the ball. The model can be used to

identify and analyze important opportunities during a match ... to assist opposition analysis by highlighting the regions of the pitch where specific players or teams are more likely to create off-ball scoring opportunities ... and to automate talent identification by finding the players across an entire league that are most proficient at creating off-ball scoring opportunities.[2]

Even with this innovative model, however, further questions are immediately raised. How was the space into which the player arrived created, for example? One attempt to model this key element of the game was conducted by the Barcelona Innovation Hub on the creation and exploitation of space.[3] The authors of the report acknowledge the value of advanced machine learning when they state that the level of detail we can reach with automated quantitative analysis of space dynamics is beyond what can be reached through observational analysis. The capacity of evaluating space occupation and generation opens the door for new research on off-ball dynamics that can be applied in specific matches and situations, and directly integrated into coaches' analysis.[4]

Of course, it is simpler to apply high tech when focusing on "one versus one" sports, such as tennis and boxing. In boxing, for example, boxers' gloves can be fitted with sensors to complement the biometric data or computer vision plus the machine learning capacity that AI provides. The sensors, which can include such technologies as accelerometers and gyroscopes, can collect and categorize as many as 40,000 data points per second on key factors such as the speed of delivery and retraction of the punch, the impact, the quantity and even the quality of the punches.

During one piece of research, carried out jointly by academics at the French National Institute of Sport, Expertise and Performance, Sport, Expertise and Performance Lab in Paris and the Research Institute for Sport and Exercise Sciences, Liverpool John Moores University, each boxer wore 17 inertial measurement units (IMUs) while delivering three commonly used punches (cross, hook and uppercut). The IMU sensors were able to calculate linear velocity, stability and punch forces. The results could then be assessed by coaches and biometric analysts for differences in joint contributions, i.e., how much the puncher uses the joint to deliver the punch. That could then be compared to their use of the relative positioning of their feet when delivering the punch. Such results have, as the authors state,

important implications for practitioners involved in the talent identification process, longitudinal follow-up, and training of boxers.[5]

These programs use AI not only to learn from the fighter but also to compare and contrast that data with other fighters generically and specifically concerning future opponents. There is also a growing market for AI-supported training bot such as Bot Boxer,[6] a glorified AI-enabled punch bag which can be used for coaching purposes without a human coach being involved (such as during a pandemic).

Within sport, wearable technology powered by AI has almost become de rigueur. Previously, biometric research, particularly, has been hampered by the need to capture data either by post activity viewing of video or by carrying out experiments in laboratory situations. Wearable technology is able to not only avoid the need to review data post event or to use a laboratory but to collect and disseminate data in real time.

Most sports now use Global Positioning System (GPS) devices to measure activities such as energy expenditure, distances covered and at which speed, as the action is occurring. As discussed earlier, sensors can also be located in players' helmets and mouthguards to measure the acceleration and deceleration of head movements to monitor concussion. AI is thus able to provide data that may otherwise be difficult to obtain, and this is true of the complete range of body movements, including but not restricted to ears, chest, wrist, lower back, thighs, head, arms, quads, ankles and, of course, feet and the shoes that cover them.

As early as 2012, Nike launched what it referred to as a smart shoe that could measure steps, how long each foot was off the ground and where/when the contact with the surface was reconnected. Most recently, the latest Nike smart shoe (the Vaporfly) has caused a furor amid charges of technological doping, not dissimilar to the 2008 controversy around Speedo's hi-tech LZR Racer swimsuit. Not surprisingly, uproar only arose when both technologies proved successful and led to multiple world records.

TOWARD REAL-TIME MEASUREMENTS

A key development for any sport would be the ability to utilize available data in real time, thus assisting coaches, athletes and officials to make decisions during the game itself. The use of HawkEye technology, first used in a cricket match 20 years ago, has become ubiquitous at the elite level. The everyday amateur's versions such as In/Out, a GoPro-like device works using similar algorithms to those used in driverless cars. Other examples of systems already in use include real-time tracking using wireless signaling to time the start and finish of races to within ±0.4 thousandths of a second.

Real-time player tracking, which tends to rely on radio systems and GPS in conjunction with wearables (e.g., player vests/tracking tags) is increasingly available. Ideally, the tracking of players directly from broadcast video footage has democratized technology because such footage can be available to every professional sports match and does, therefore, avoid the need for bespoke sensory modules.

In cricket, the amount of information collectible simply from data generated by sensors on the bat is available to educate players and coaches is impressive. AI is able to assist in the measurement of the speed of the bat at the moment of impact, for example, which determines the power of a shot; the twist of the bat, which can determine the deviation between the intended and the actual direction of the shot based on the degree of rotation of the bat on impact with the ball; the location of that impact, where the ball makes contact with the bat, measured in relation to the "sweet spot" of the bat; and the swing angles of the bat, which measures such factors as the angles of backlift, bat face angle, downswing angle, launch angle of the bat at the instant of ball impact and the follow-through angle.

In the National Hockey League (NHL), the league itself initiated the drive to enable all teams to have access to real-time data. According to the SVP of business development and innovation at the time (2017), Dave Lehanski, the impetus for change came from the coaches and GMs who wanted access to smarter and more immediate in-game data and analytics,

> For years they'd been using it prior and post-game to analyse the performance of the team to evaluate players, to scout, to evaluate trades, but the growing desire was to use it during the game.[7]

He added that

> Now, coaches can get real-time data and analytics on an iPad Pro behind the bench during every game of the season … we're able to deliver that data within a few seconds, so literally as players are coming off the ice, they're grabbing the iPad and looking at what happened only a few seconds ago and can get instant feedback on their performance.

What the NHL has done differently, though, is to ensure that instead of allowing each team access to game data in its own configuration, it has protected the competitive balance by ensuring that,

> all the teams have access to that type of data and to those [same] solutions.

The greater availability of wearable technology for individuals, teams, coaches at both professional and amateur levels, has been accelerated by the Covid-19 pandemic. The downloading of fitness apps, for example, has risen by approximately 60%. The democratizing effect of AI on the sports industry is key to driving returns on investment and ensuring a continual flow of research funding.

AI AND STRATEGY

While AI has been increasingly efficient at learning from discrete events, developing, predicting and implementing strategies present yet another level of complexity. In road race cycling, for example, the communication channels used by every team must be able to seamlessly support a huge logistical operation not only for sharing real-time information on such issues as the road surface conditions, but also for the development of in-race adjustments and strategies.

In the Tour de France, each management team has to communicate with eight riders, and there may be as many as 25 separate teams. Simple logistics such as agreeing each team's unique radio frequency so that other teams cannot listen to the communications of competitors is essential. Of course, with modern hacking capabilities, the process of frequency allocation may not be as simple as in the past.

Assuming that hurdle is surmounted, then comms with team vehicles, support vehicles from the Tour organizers, press motorcycles on the road and the fact that the riders are riding kilometers apart, especially on mountain stages, implies that a perfectly functioning communication system is essential to the success of the race.

In his interesting article on strategies in elite road racing, Mignot posited that the

> strategic interactions of riders have the same logical structure as many social interactions. Among the multiple games within the larger game of bicycle races are: games between two individuals (riders) or organizations (teams), but also games among three or more players, which allow coalitions to develop; games that are constant-sum or variable-sum, thus involving partly conflicting interests but also potentially mutually beneficial cooperation; games that are simultaneous or sequential, thus allowing players to (mis)trust each other and be (dis)loyal; and games that involve complete or incomplete information, allowing players to screen others, signal their unobservable characteristics or bluff.[8]

As with the complexity problems posed by football, so too the complexity of road race cycling provides an excellent game-theoretic crucible for research. Much more so than in swimming or running sprints on the track or even the zero-sum games like boxing, fencing, martial arts or tennis. Whether it is deciding if/when to slipstream or when to attack, be it during a mountain stage or a flat stage, or indeed, which specific stage in the overall race might be best to attack, the complexity is daunting. Similarly, decisions must be made about cooperation with other riders in a breakaway situation or within the peloton or whether to cooperate at all. There are also n-player interactions to consider, with whom should a rider ally and against whom?

When, where and how to sprint is yet another strategic decision to be made. All of the above assume a rider is riding to win, yet many riders are "domestiques" or "gregari" whose job descriptions are simply, "helping the team leader" to win. The sheer variety of strategic options provides the type of AI challenges and opportunities that are needed to advance AI capabilities. Using ML techniques, predictive models can be trained to enable sampling of a multitude of viable proposals using historical strategies (and success rates thereof) as learning targets; the models can then generate proposed strategies for the team managers to consider, ranked by their estimated value to the team, and ideally communicated in a manner that is interpretable by the decision-making humans – possibly the most difficult hurdle to surmount.

OFFICIATING IN AN AI WORLD

One aspect of sports often neglected is how they are officiated. Augmented refereeing and fine-tuning the game rules are crucial to both the aesthetic and commercial well-being of the games. Just as it is now possible to measure the time of the 100 meters final to thousandths of a second, so too can VAR (Virtual Assistant Referee) aid the human referee in football. Notwithstanding the teething problems of the system, only implemented in 2018, VAR is here to stay and improvements with the controversial offside capabilities of the system, for example, are already in progress.

The FIFA-certified virtual offside line (VOL) system is in the process of being semi-automated, and then fully automated, such that the referee will get immediate decisions sent to wearable technology in the same way as goal-line technology currently enables. Of course, the problem with automating offside technology is the difficulty of coordinating the instance of impact on the ball by the pass deliverer and the position of the alleged encroacher, which is the hurdle now being worked on by the AI community.

The technology under test is using tracking data from sensor technology and/or video data for the coordination. In accurately positioning the potentially offside player, the issue is for the AI program to precisely isolate the relevant body part, always assuming that the lawmakers can agree on that. If/when they do, the AI technology will provide algorithms that can identify which body part placed the player offside and by what distance. A statement from IFAB (International Football Association Board) makes it clear that the system will be a proposer, not a decider:

> The goal is to develop a supportive tool similar to goal-line technology: Not designed to make the decision, but to provide evidence instantly to the referees.[9]

The success of the officiating in the recent Euros confirmed that the best system is a cooperative relationship between machine and human.

As automated assistance to the referees becomes the accepted practice, more innovations will quickly emerge, which is not uncommon with technological development. The general acceptance of artificial playing surfaces, for example, has been significantly delayed because of the rejection of the idea itself as a result of the disastrous early attempts. The advantages that AI/ML provides when compared to human referees are powerful but often resisted, leading to slower but ultimately inevitable implementation.

The natural resistance of humans to passing responsibility to a machine for major life decisions is well documented in instances such as automatic pilots and driverless cars, and the same appears true with our major cultural passions such as sport. Appropriately trained automated systems do not have off-days, they do not have "blind spots" and limited attention, they do not have to be physically fit and they do not grow old because they can be continuously upgraded.

Of course, the natural question is what constitutes "appropriate training" for a machine, especially considering the variety of inappropriately trained AI systems deployed in both sports settings which can make biased decisions, ultimately negatively and disproportionately impacting some portion of the user population.

Ideally, automation will not only help make judgment calls appear fairer to players, teams and fans but also make them comparable across different matches, thus ensuring that globally everyone is being judged on an equal platform. This is especially key for the more subjectively judged sports such as gymnastics, figure skating, diving and synchronized swimming, indeed any sport where aesthetics is judged.

Of course, it has to be recognized that the introduction of more accurate decisions may also change the dynamics of the game itself. For example, physical tactics can change due to stricter enforcement of rules; more psychological tactics such as simulation (diving) or player-ref arguments may well disappear if there is clear objective evidence from a well-trained system that the players cannot refute. It may even lead to tactical changes in playing styles. The success of football teams heavily reliant on AI-supported analytics such as Brentford may also lead to copycat stylistic changes.

New or better-enforced rules will always lead to better-informed tactics to defeat the officiators, be they human or machine. And that includes attacks from the betting industry. In volleyball, *VideoCheck* provides data extracted from high-speed cameras to detect fouls and faults delivered instantly to the referee. The Brazilian volleyball governing body, CBV, has constructed a deal with *Genius Sports*, a leader in sports data technology, for the company to hold exclusive rights for the collection and distribution of its official data and simultaneously monitor integrity and official data strategy aimed at combating match-fixing and data piracy. Genius Sports' *Bet Monitoring System* will deliver betting intelligence on all global betting markets relevant to all CBV competitions utilizing the data accumulated as a consequence of the control of the official data to which it now has exclusive access.

In one of the more subjective sports, gymnastics, there has been significant progress in recent years in partnership with the Fujitsu Corporation. Fujitsu has developed AI and 3D sensor technology that assists gymnastic performance judging.

The technology, called the *Judging Support System*, utilizes AI and 3D sensors to capture each gymnast's movement before analyzing it as numerical data, primarily for confirming difficulty scores. The system is used by the judges in conjunction with the *Instant Replay and Control System* (IRCOS), a standard video replay system nearly 20 years old.

The system provides a 3D view of the performance using a variety of selections for angle measurements that can, for example, eliminate a judge's inaccurate assessment of body angles calculated for technical difficulty purposes (Figure 7.1).

The FIG (Fédération Internationale de Gymnastique) president Morinari Watanabe has said,

> The people we must always have in mind are the gymnasts.…
> Scoring controversies must become a thing of the past, and the technology that Fujitsu has developed [with us] will reinforce trust in judgement.[10]

Naturally, while such technology enables judges to be more consistent across issues of fact, that is only one element of the judging criteria where matters of style and aesthetics still remain within the human domain.

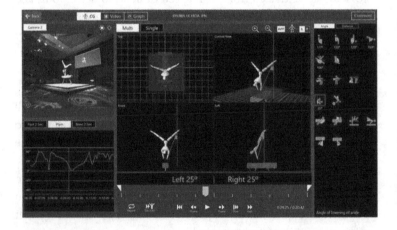

Figure 7.1 Screenshots of Fujitsu's Judging Support System. Image: Fujitsu.

NOTES

1. Actions Speak Louder than Goals: Valuing Player Actions in Soccer (arxiv.org).

2. https://www.google.com/url?q=https://dl.acm.org/doi/10.1145/32 92500.3330758&sa=D&source=editors&ust=1622720253000&us g=AOvVaw3TtunutlpC1sVXkBux0UEd

3. *Wide Open Spaces: A statistical technique for measuring space creation in professional soccer.* Javier Fernandez F.C. Barcelona javier.fernandez@fcbarcelona.cat; Luke Bornn Simon Fraser University, Sacramento Kings lbornn@sfu.ca

4. Ibid.

5. *Frontiers in Sports Act.* Living, 26 November 2020 | https://doi.org/10.3389/ fspor.2020.598861; *Biomechanical Analysis of the Cross, Hook, and Uppercut in Junior vs. Elite Boxers: Implications for Training and Talent Identification* by Daniel Dinu and Julien Louis.

6. https://botboxer.com/

7. How the NHL is planning on using data analytics to change the game for everyone | ZDNet.

8. Jean-François Mignot. *Strategic behaviour in road cycling competitions.* The Economics of Professional Road Cycling, pp. 207–31, 2016.

9. https://www.fifa.com/who-we-are/news/fifa-organises-remote-demonstration-of-advanced-offside-technology

10. Fujitsu's AI to help judges score gymnastic performances at World Championships | ZDNet; for an interesting article on the views of participants in elite gymnastics go to – Computerised gymnastics judging scoring system implementation – an exploration of stakeholders' perceptions – University of Salford Institutional Repository, A. Fenton et al.

8

AI *AROUND* THE GAME

DATA COLLECTION CHALLENGES

Any modernization encounters obstacles. There are genuine player worries about privacy and health. As with all data, they are concerned about how it will be used. Performance data, for example, could be abused by agents and clubs to influence contractual negotiations over pay and terms and conditions.

Also, too much distributed data can be infrastructurally difficult to work with, as mentioned by R.C. Buford, CEO of the San Antonio Spurs, during an interview with the authors,

> We've got all this data in 100 different places, and everyone is saying we have it; but do we really have [it], or is it living in 5 or 10 different environments? It's an infrastructure issue first ... too many information systems do not talk well enough to each other, and we have to ask the questions we want answered, rather than [the system] coming to us and telling us the questions we may not be asking.

Current collection methods are expensive (further fueling the need for machine learning [ML]-driven automated data collection schemes). Ownership of, and access to, data can also be problematic (especially for academics and research scientists). One solution

DOI: 10.1201/9781003196532-11

is that taken by the *National Football League Players Association* (NFLPA), which recently completed a deal with the health wearable company *WHOOP* such that the players own the individual data collected by the *WHOOP* technology. As owners they are then able to monetize their personal data if they so wish.

Similar data protection issues are inevitable as artificial intelligence (AI) systems for scouting, coaching and tactical decision-making continue to improve. Certain legal principles such as those covered by the European Data Protection Regulation (GDPR) will need clarification. Privacy, for example, accuracy of data, data minimization and transparency in data movement will become more obviously important issues. Also, the individual athlete's consent is required prior to the processing of any data which can, as in the WHOOP/NFLPA deal, always be negotiated, although those negotiations will never be easy. Neither will the regulations regarding the special category of health-related data, the use of which is not permitted without the "explicit consent" of the individual. Compliance becomes a significant cost center for the organization.

THE MONEY GAME

Trying to dissociate the sport itself from the business of sport is a hapless task. It is, after all, the love and passion for the games that drive the businesses. The sports market has now reached a valuation in the region of $400 billion on the back of a consistent CAGR (compound annual growth rate) close to 5% since 2014.[1] By 2022, it was expected, prior to Covid-19, to hit circa $600 billion depending upon which analyst was consulted. What is not in dispute is that the industry is growing faster than the global GDP.

The industry valuation includes the games themselves plus revenue from the commercial aspects such as catering, memorabilia, replica kit sales, image rights, major construction projects, and that super-growth engine, broadcasting. It does not include sports betting, which adds another estimated $200 billion to the pot.

In reality, the sports industry is omnipresent as an industry and generates revenue from two macro-segments: taking part and watching. Taking part would include playing, general fitness activities, leisure centers, local golf clubs, gyms, personal training and the scope goes on. Spectator (watching) revenue comes from the games and the associated stadiums and content exploitation revenue such as that directly from events, media rights, sponsorship, merchandising and gambling. The two major segments split the pie almost 50/50, although the spectator segment is expected to provide the fastest growth over the post-Covid decade.

The one common denominator in each segment is the fan. The fan provides the rationale for each of the traditional revenue streams – match day, commercial, broadcasting. Without the fan, there is no business; there is sport but no business. The sport itself will always exist, but the business needs the fans and AI is fast becoming a major factor in the fan experience. The most important sports in terms of revenue are association football and gridiron football, which together account for more than half the market. While there is much discussion as to the sustainability of football as the dominant sports business, there is little evidence of an early decline.

Where and how does AI intersect with this huge fan-related element of the market? The development and growth of digital technology driven by AI and ML in particular includes innovative streaming services, virtual reality, etc. The expansion of digital gambling platforms is also inevitable as US sports betting legislation softens.

At the back end of July 2021, Caesars Entertainment launched Caesars Sportsbook, its new mobile sports betting app. Tom Reeg, Caesars' CEO, is convinced that online revenues from sports betting and igaming would be fairly evenly split and Caesars need to be competing in both markets. He expects to invest as much as $1 billion during the next two/three years to establish a powerful online customer base. Caesars currently operate sportsbooks in 17 states, 13 of which offer mobile sports betting. Reeg believes that they can generate cash-on-cash returns in this business at maturity well in excess of fifty percent of what we'll invest.[2]

With such returns, it is difficult to imagine that digital gambling will do anything other than grow at a pace and that AI will power that growth.

Esports is another growing presence that will continue to expand with the development of more sophisticated VR technology, which in combination with AI can enable the interaction of humans with machine counterparts in a virtual setting. In 2020, global Esports revenues reached the billion-dollar mark, which represents a year-on-year growth of approximately 16%, on the previous year. Of that revenue, as much as 80% derives from media rights and sponsorship.

Global Esports audience revenues are now close to $500 million with annual growth rates of 10%.[3] China, North America and Western Europe currently dominate the revenue tables with smaller nations such as South Korea having higher rates of players per population. In those large markets, major league clubs are creating their own Esports division, absorbing established teams or partnering with developing teams. The association can help to feed engagement for the regular fan. The Phoenix Suns, for example, simulated its remaining 2020 regular-season games on NBA 2K, streamed on Twitch for the fans unable to visit the arena during Covid-19. The Esports Twitch stream of the parallel e-version of the scheduled game against the Dallas Mavericks drew more than 200,000 views.

However, by far the strongest growth revenue generator in the sports industry is the gambling sector. The global sports betting industry has reached a market size of over $2 billion and is projected to grow to $8 billion in the next five years. This growth is fueled by the legalization of gambling in many if not most US states.

THE FANS

Who are these modern fans and what do they want that AI can help to provide? Although they are digital fans, *homo digitalis*, they are first and foremost sports fans. Irrespective as to where they are placed on the spectrum between those who are engaged every day and those who engage once a year, from the strongly identified to weakly identified, they are fans. For the strongly identified fans, sport is central to their identity. For example, 95% of these fans currently have some form of interaction with their favorite team or league in the off-season.[4] They need to stay attached. And why is that important? Because those who engage just once a month in the off-season tend to spend 40% more than fans who have no engagement during the off-season.

When they are staying in touch with "their team" outside the arena, what is it that they value the most? Number one appears to be the quality of the broadcast or stream and the control they have over that stream for such aspects as the ability to select particular screens or, in Covid times, stadium noise (real or artificial). The true enthusiast also spends three times more than casual fans on streaming and 1.5 times more than casual fans on the broadcast. Fan media is now part of the event narrative and is on an irreversible growth trajectory. During the last FIFA World Cup, for example, nearly 700 million tweets were sent. The volume of fan-generated content is demanding new outlets such as *Twitter Moments, Snapchat Stories* and myriad others.

Fans are no longer passive consumers of sporting content; they demand participation to the extent that, with Formula E's *FanBoost* technology, fans can literally boost a driver's chances of success via their cell phones. The fan can now compete against their professional heroes through social networks such as *Strava* and *Runkeeper* (GPS fitness-tracking apps), which allow them to retrace their routes and see how their times compare. The fan can literally ride the exact same route as their heroes' ride, either in races or in training. Of course, this is the classic two-way street of social media. While the cyclists are riding to compete against their digital competitors, they are simultaneously providing data to *Strava* that it can use to sell to town planners about traffic conditions and times, for example. As these simulations become more sophisticated, they may also become platforms to train and recruit future managers and transfer that learning to corporate HR functions.

As a consequence of burgeoning digital developments, an action as simple as improving the broadcast experience can increase fan satisfaction and drive better returns. Most estimates put the statistics at more than 60% of fans who agree that top-quality broadcast experiences lead to becoming more engaged with the team, more likely to watch and attend a game, and nearly 40% feel closer to team sponsors, whatever "closer" might mean in this context.[5]

These are known desires, but they are desires that are not well serviced, satisfied and only slowly understood. Fans are now referred to as space-shifters in that they can move digital assets from one platform to another, which, although that might be considered copyright infringement in certain cases, has nonetheless become a common practice among the digital generation. In non-sports environments such as drama, consumers can also time-shift, i.e., watch content when/where they choose. More than a third of consumers time-shift general content, whereas with sports content that number is less than 7%. Two-thirds of ESPN's audience is exclusively mobile. No surprise then that telecoms and internet corporations are investing heavily in sports content and delivery.

The same survey showed that overall satisfaction with the broadcast experience was only 39%. This is where enhanced AI can deliver an upgraded technological experience for fans by converging and integrating augmented reality (AR), virtual reality (VR), social media and gambling into a complete viewing experience. An IBM survey on the future of the sports fan found that a significant majority of fans wanted to be able to access content more simply. The enthusiasts know what they want, and they want it now.

Already, the growth in AR/VR as must-haves for the affluent fan base is big business. According to *Statista.com*, the global AR and VR market is now close to $20 billion. In 2020, sales of AR/VR headsets reached 5.5 million units with Sony's *PlayStation* VR and Facebook's *Oculus VR* headsets taking the vast majority of the market.[6] VR headsets are becoming increasingly popular among gamers, and as they become more sophisticated, they will be an important factor in the fan experience, albeit only of those fans able to afford them.

At Manchester City Football Club, VR has been used to enhance training methods but also to significantly improve the fan experience. Prior to its unfortunate demise, *Jaunt VR* showcased a 360 VR experience for the club, which included access to the players' locker room and a close-up view of the players arriving on the blue carpet which had over 1 million views in the first few days after release. As Diego Gigliani of the City Football Group told the press,

> Although there's nothing that compares with attending a match at the Etihad Stadium, the emergence of 360 video and virtual reality has allowed us to capture some of that atmosphere and excitement in ways that weren't possible in the past.

That was 3 years ago, and the technology does not stand still. *Immersive. io*, a company whose products are fundamentally underpinned by AI, has created a "robust AI for [their] Sports Augmented Reality (AR) Experience".[7] The product, *ARISE*, provides a real-time experience, with what is visible on the field being digitally translated into real-time statistics mapped on to the consumer's technology with minimal lag time using, among other things, *5G Edge Computing*. Deep learning is enabling fully automated sports production that is difficult to distinguish from traditional "real" broadcasting content. AI-driven cameras are as efficient at identifying key moments in a game, such as baskets or goals and automatically producing highlight clips, as any human camera operator and much better at instantly delivering them to TV, streaming or mobile devices. And the computer vision technology supporting such products is fast becoming one of the most lucrative global technology markets with projected revenue close to $20 billion by 2027.

For the flow of content to fans to remain effective, however, the dosage has to be increased and this is achieved by customizing and curating content and delivering real-time stats accompanied by chatbots attached to promotions, sales of season tickets and other VIP subscriptions and merchandise. Mobile apps can also easily enable advanced ordering from concessions stands. Bizarrely, nearly half of fans in a recent Deloitte's survey indicated that the presence of real-time augmented reality stats on stadium screens would increase their likelihood of watching a live game – who knew?

A significant finding of other recent research is that engagement with fantasy sports makes fans more likely to watch games on television and even to attend them in person. Perhaps confirming the thesis that it is sport that is the medicine and the manner in which it is administered can be as diverse as the fans themselves.

Dr. Alex Fenton, editor of *Strategic Digital Transformation*, explains the interconnection within the digital sports fan's ecosystem through Figure 8.1.[8]

His conclusion is that the interaction and consequent interdependency of all aspects of the system cannot be underestimated either within the stadiums or outside the stadiums. It is difficult, for example, to imagine any major sports organization not having its own dedicated app connecting the club and the fan to a global network. Chelsea Football Club's app, "The 5th stand" as an example, allows fans to find and then connect with other fan forums. It also provides fantasy league advice, quizzes and polls. Every capability that smartphones possess, such as their cameras and microphones, is also being used to engage fans. It is the communication channel of choice – for the moment.

IN-STADIUM FAN EXPERIENCE

Irrespective of the merits of remote consumption of sporting content, visits to stadiums are still prime experiences for all fans, weak or strong. Innovative technologies are also becoming omnipresent within modern stadiums and, in fact, becoming a central part of the design and construction planning process of new stadiums. Controlling the arrival of fans through the turnstiles or moving fans toward concession stands, advertising visuals, either physically or while sitting in their seats is now commonplace.

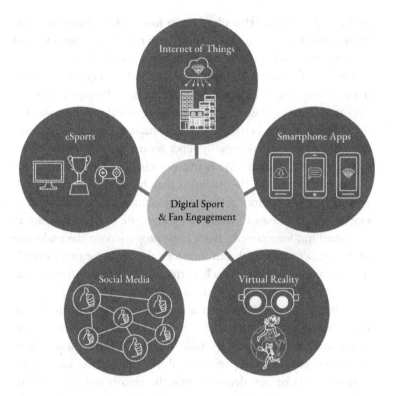

Figure 8.1 Digital sport and fan engagement. (*Source:* Adapted from *Strategic Digital Transformation*)

Sports organizations are already well advanced in their adoption of automated entry into the stadiums. Liverpool FC, for example, has linked with *Near Field Communication* (NFC) technology to provide contactless entry to Anfield as soon as Covid permits.[9] Fans who do not have access to mobile phones and/or NFC technology will be able to use a card with a photographic ID to enter the stadium.

Once in the stadium, fans can access a plethora of data predominantly on their personal digital devices. In the Levi Stadium,[10] for example, during Super Bowl 50 in 2016, 10 terabytes of data were transferred over the stadium's connections. The majority of that data traveled through the San Francisco 49ers official app. Fans were able to simultaneously watch replays, order food and be guided not only to the nearest toilets but also to those with the shortest queues – and the 49ers were able to collect and analyze all of that data.

Once the fans had found how to order food through the app, they did so to the tune of an average of $88 per head. Perhaps even more important than the revenue, if that is possible, would have been the data the app collected on behaviors that can enable the machines to learn and improve fan experiences. By Super Bowl 2018, 70% of the crowd logged on to the stadium's Wi-Fi and the technology did not fail once.[11]

Even attendance at the stadiums may become a hybrid experience as fans who cannot get into the stadium (if already sold out or empty, e.g., because of Covid) can congregate outside. Barcelona's new stadium, for example, has a large projection on the underside of the arena's roof which can broadcast the game (or other events) to fans outside. Fan zones such as that at the Etihad will grow and prosper in terms of fan satisfaction and revenue.

In the hinterland between the physical and virtual fan experiences lies Cryptocurrency land. An early innovation involves a fan engagement token which is "fully fungible". These tokens allow their owners to directly vote on club matters such as kit designs, naming rights or any decisions that the club is willing to share. Other benefits such as VIP access and exclusive early access to certain events and havens are also available.

There are also "non-fungible tokens" (NFT). These tokens, which might include items such as sports cards, can be stored in digital wallets. An NFT is best understood as a method of establishing proof of ownership of an asset verified by the blockchain. The emergence of *CryptoPunks*, a collection of thousands of unique art characters that can be "owned", with that ownership verified by the Ethereum blockchain, as recently as 2017, presaged the way for the development of other NFTs such as, in sports, trading cards. To provide a snapshot of the scale of this crypto environment, in March 2021, a *CryptoPunks* sold for 4,200 Ethereum or the equivalent of more than $7 million.

In 2019, the NBA signed a deal with *Dapper Labs*, a company that packages "moments" (e.g., famous video clips from NBA games) for trading on the crypto collectibles market to deliver the NBA's hugely successful *Top Shot* service, a blockchain-based trading card system. The service is claimed to have already generated more than $200 million in gross sales. The NBA (and the NBAPA) licenses the "moments" to *Dapper Laps*, which digitizes the footage, making only a limited amount to create scarcity. In that way, the market works very much like a traditional trading card market but without the risk of damage or theft of the asset.

As far back as 2014, the sponsorship opportunities provided by an aspiration technology such as crypto currencies were recognized by the sports sector, US-bitcoin payment processor *BitPay* and ESPN Events, for example, sponsored an annual post-season college football game as part of the deal to promote *Bitcoin*. Such sponsorship has grown apace with *CashBet Coin*'s sponsorship of Arsenal Football Club, LiteCoin sponsoring a UFC title fight and eToro, the financial trading platform, engaging with at least six English Premier League clubs with a view to providing services such as authentication of merchandise, a reduction in ticket touting and cleaning up player transfer activity – all underwritten by *Bitcoin*. Blockchain technologies have also enabled more secure and transparent ticket exchange markets, a long-needed service. However, *caveat emptor*, not only are trading markets naturally volatile but trading markets using crypto currencies may well be doubly so.

EXTRA-STADIUM FAN EXPERIENCE

AI has taken on a key role in informing the fans about the whole spectrum of activities in which their clubs and the sports are engaged. It has aided the development of *automated broadcasting, commentary and journalism*, for example, which use computer vision technologies to automatically create content. This involves understanding and tracking where the "action" in a game is. Rather than having a camera being carried around the field of play by an operator, a system such as *Spiideo's* intelligent camera system and cloud platform automatically captures the entire field at all times. The system automatically identifies where the action is taking place and continues to follow it based on the algorithmic training with which the system has been provided.

Ever-more capable (and portable) cameras are also in use that may eventually contribute to the democratization of sports analytics. Although designed through a collaboration between two major organizations (*Barcelona FC* and *Pixellot*), the camera produced by that collaboration can be easily used by any size club to record any sporting activities, and through AI they can track any game situation based on player and ball movements. These can instantaneously be converted into highlight reels based on the previously agreed-upon targeted actions selected by the coaches and/or analysts and maybe even sold as NFTs.

Another development powered by AI is in the media coverage of the sports. In cricket, for example, deep neural networks are now capable of generating commentary on the match by just observing it. An English reader will understand, of course, that nothing can replace the conversations about "tea-time cakes" in the BBC's Test Match Special (TMS) studios – yet.[12]

In baseball, the Associated Press has been working with AI since 2016 using their proprietary *Wordsmith AI* platform "to turn Minor League Baseball game data into stories that go straight to the wire".[13] *Wordsmith* is a Natural Language Generator (NLG), but like the GPT-3 system created by *OpenAI*, it is far from the finished product. Both systems can automatically produce human sounding language quickly. However, both can also produce quite obviously ludicrous statements. Even the CEO of *OpenAI*, Sam Altman, is quoted as saying that,

> The GPT-3 hype is way too much. It's impressive … but it still has serious weaknesses and sometimes makes very silly

mistakes. AI is going to change the world, but GPT-3 is just an early glimpse. We have a lot to figure out.[14]

As Altman points out, there is little doubt that AI will change the world, but there will be obstacles and setbacks along the way and these setbacks should not be allowed to create another AI winter.

ADVERTISING AND MARKETING

Advertising and marketing seek to deliver positively packaged information to current or potential consumers and, just as importantly, receive information from that same source. For example, brand recognition is a key strategic metric for any organization, and sports organizations are especially sensitive to how fans and other consumers view them. By using techniques from computer vision, tech companies can now measure brand recognition more accurately.

Companies such as the Israeli-based *vBrand*, now part of the *Neilson* corporation, use advanced image recognition technology combined with AI and deep learning to analyze whenever a sponsor's logo is visible to the human eye. They do this by identifying logos as a result of literally frame-by-frame logo recognition from standard TV, digital TV, web and social media sources. From that data, they calculate sponsorship opportunities and brand valuations using weighted specifics such as duration, size and image clarity.

This is a clear example of the immediate added value of AI in the heavy lifting role where the workload can be increased as necessary. For example, the AI platform can identify emotions through face recognition, it can seek actions, activities, copyright infringements, image rights infringements and a variety of other factors for the human analysts to deconstruct and interpret in due course. Digital marketing and digital communication have become essential components of the marketing landscape for consumers of sports, both in stadiums and at home. AI provides that consumption with maximum related information.

Prior to the onset of the Covid pandemic, the Tokyo Olympics were expected to see the most significant breakthrough in the public recognition of the benefits of virtual reality, augmented reality and mixed reality to enhance the fan experience. Opportunities for the 3D tracking of athletes screened in stadiums as well as easily accessible data on the profile of individual athletes.

In terms of security, AI-based facial recognition software is now able to identify more than 300,000 people within various arenas, which naturally comes with a variety of legal and ethical considerations that are being explored by researchers and policymakers. The 2020 Olympics was on course to be an AI-enabled spectacle given that Japan is already at the forefront of AI-based technological innovation. The pandemic may actually have accelerated the progress, but only time will ultimately tell.

GAMBLING

As reports of allegations against athletes in most sports are regularly published, it is a reminder of the dangers posed by one of the biggest financial beneficiaries of the global sports industry – the gambling sector. Players at that level of the game are mostly chasing their dreams at a financial loss and are therefore vulnerable to the temptations dangled by unscrupulous gambling syndicates.

However, sport and gambling have always been inextricably linked. From the earliest days of cricket in the late 1700s right through to the Hansie Cronje scandal of the 2000s and from the Black Sox and Pete Rose scandals in baseball to whatever/whoever is involved in the next one, gambling scandals are seemingly inevitable. But, as the sponsorship of English Premier League football clubs by betting companies shows, sports and gambling are difficult to disentangle.

Sports betting is a huge market, and a tantalizing one for owners and broadcasters because fans who participate in gambling may as a result of that participation also be or become engaged in wider sports (e.g., start watching games beyond those of their teams, or even sports they might not otherwise watch). The role of AI/ML in sports also throws up an interesting dynamic. On the one hand, AI/ML seeks to minimize uncertainty; on the other hand, the gambling fraternity seeks to profit from it.

Sports betting actually provides an interesting insight into the strengths of AI as a product that enhances the symbiosis between machines and humans. The AI system underpinning the successful *Sportspicker* AI betting prediction service, *Swarm*, works on a quite simple model. As its website explains,

> Sportspicker AI uses Swarm AI technology to harness the knowledge, wisdom, insights, and intuition of real people (sports fans) in real-time, generating forecasts that have been shown to outperform other methods.[15]

This sounds very much like a fairly simplistic and well-controlled job for AI – to do the heavy lifting of sifting and identifying trends from data input into the machine. In this case, the data is the product of human knowledge. As an example, one of the authors of this book, a self-confessed movie nerd, comfortably outperformed the *Unanimous AI* 2021 Oscar predictions. The 93% success rate highlighted on the company website was not difficult to achieve given the relatively small numbers in the Oscar categories.

However, with the sheer volume and complexity of the data available for Sports Book betting, the heavy lifting can be truly *heavy!* Companies like *UnanimousAI* and *Predictology*[16] are, simply put, AI-powered tipster services precluded from disadvantaging the punter, given that their results and consequent returns will be as good as they can be while still limited by the laws of probability. However, the fact remains that the thing that ultimately drives the passion for sports is its unpredictability, so, good luck predicting the future. One prediction that we will make is that if machines one day can imitate human intelligence, they will still bet on the wrong horse.

Notwithstanding the unpredictable nature of the sports themselves, the one thing that is predictable is that gambling companies make their profits from sports as do the ancillary organizations which provide services to the bookies in the same way that products are supplied to any front-line retailer.

What makes gambling and its supply chain so profitable is not the margins but the scale. In April 2021, for example, a British sports betting data group went public on the NYSE after a $1.5 billion merger with the dMY *Technology Group, Inc. II*, a special-purpose acquisition company (SPAC). *Genius Sports*, the official provider of data to the NFL, and its SPAC partner are making the move as the US sports betting market opens up with the relaxation of anti-gambling legislation. With the United States finally joining the rest of the world, the sports gambling sector can only continue to grow.

The difficulty in accurately assessing just how big the sports betting market is lies in the fact that more than 50% of it is illegal and does not, therefore, show up in official figures.[17] However, to give an indication of its size, most estimates put the total global gambling market at $200 billion+ with the online market, including fantasy sports betting, at around $70 billion.

THE CURRENT STATE

All major sports now incorporate AI into all aspects of their sporting and business models. However, the quantity and quality of the AI integration is variable both within and between sports as diverse as football, with its huge complexity and billions of potential data points, and snooker/pool where AI programs can animate shots, suggest possible angles and cannons, show potting distances or ball pathways. In NASCAR, auto industry giants partner with AI companies to help them deliver driverless cars to the retail and corporate market and then spin that knowledge back to the track to make racing a safer proposition. The machines can now identify a car and/or a driver nearing a malfunction episode during a race quicker than can the humans, thus making the race track a safer place for competitors and spectators alike.

Within the health sector, AI is being engaged during operations as well as in a prevention mode for injuries and illnesses through wearable technology. Fans are becoming activists as well as consumers of experiences and content both inside and outside the stadiums. And the stadiums in which they do engage directly with their teams are morphing into multimedia entertainment centers.

The sports gambling sector is also growing exponentially, fueled by AI-based virtual betting shops/casinos, and with the gravitational pull of a black hole, it is pulling Esports and fantasy sports into its orbit. It is estimated that as much as $30 billion will be wagered on Esports by 2022. Within the game, the feedback loop of pre/during/post-game data utilization is growing in importance when informing the recruitment, tactical analysis, coaching, playing and officiating sectors.

Commercially, the US sports market alone was estimated, before the Covid pandemic, to be worth $80 billion. Globally, the number is closer to $200 billion and that does not include sports betting. Revenue predominantly derives from match day, media rights, sponsorship and merchandising. Post-Covid, none of those revenue streams will be going away and the value of AI innovation to the sports industry globally will only increase, probably exponentially. What that future may look like is the subject of Part Three.

NOTES

1. https://www.businesswire.com/news/home/20190514005472/en/Sports---614-Billion-Global-Market-Opportunities-Strategies-to-2022---ResearchAndMarkets.com
2. https://www.cdcgamingreports.com/caesars-entertainment-2q-report-adds-digital-reporting-touts-post-pandemic-gains/
3. https://cardosovolei.com/rkpakn/global-games-market-report-2020-pdf
4. https://www2.deloitte.com/us/en/pages/technology-media-and-telecommunications/articles/developing-sports-marketing-strategies-year-round.html
5. Deloitte fan survey, 2020.

6. Joint research report by Performance Communications (www.performancecomms.com) and Canvas8, a market research consultancy (www.canvas8.com).

7. https://www.immersiv.io/blog/ai-sports-augmented-reality-stadium/

8. *Strategic Digital Transformation: A Results-Driven Approach* – First Edition (routledge.com).

9. https://www.liverpoolfc.com/nfc-guide

10. Levi's® Stadium – Home of the San Francisco 49ers (levisstadium.com)

11. https://www.researchgate.net/publication/266654549_Understanding_the_super-sized_traffic_of_the_super_bowl

12. For the uninitiated, it is worth going to bbc.co.uk/cricket and logging in to TMS for a weirdly British cultural experience.

13. Take Me Out to the Ball Game: Ai & AP Automate Baseball Journalism At Scale | | Automated Insights.

14. Press release 19th October 2020.

15. Sportspicker AI – UNANIMOUS AI

16. Using AI to Find Winners | Predictology.co

17. See Forbes from April 2020 (https://www.forbes.com/sites/andrewjsilver/2020/04/07/legal-sports-betting-still-faces-competition-from-illegal-market-low-state-taxes-could-turn-the-tide/) on the challenges faced by legal gambling companies from the illegal sector. This is in the United States only, but it is likely to be much worse globally.

Part 3

WHERE DO WE GO FROM HERE?

9

A FUTURE WITHIN THE GAME

The recent arrival of DeepMind's *AlphaFold2*[1] may be yet another signal along the road toward the goal of artificial general intelligence (AGI). This journey, previously evidenced by the recent successful development of what are referred to as multi-modal and multi-task models, is continual and presents futuristic predictions with an ever-changing landscape. These programs enable previously compartmentalized issues such as language (e.g., *OpenAI's* GPT-3) and imagery to be combined and dealt with simultaneously. At the time of writing (July 2021), the development of new and/or updated programs such as Google's *Multi-task Unified Model* (MUM) and the latest *WUDA* 2.0 from the Beijing Academy of Artificial Intelligence (BAAI) are accelerating at pace but also risk being upstaged by the likes of *AlphaFold* and whatever other projects are waiting in the wings.

Conventional deep learning models have been inhibited by having to be task specific. Multi-modal/task models can address completely different types of problems and for the sports industry such programs can be game changers. In the same way that the industrial revolution streamlined manufacturing, the AGI revolution will streamline information processing and enable the rapid digestion of multiple parallel data streams in a manner similar to, and possibly even beyond, human cognition.

DOI: 10.1201/9781003196532-13

This, in turn, enables the automated distillation of extremely complex data into the most salient and useful signals and insights, the objective being that humans and machines will be able talk to each other in a common language. In our view, when AGI becomes a reality, it will signal the end of one phase of the journey toward the inevitable merging of human and machine intelligence and the beginning of the next leg of that journey.

By adding the anticipated convergence of AI approaches to the potential for the convergence of different disciplines, platforms and data sources such as gamification, esports and video analyses, the resultant product should provide more holistic explanations and solutions to hitherto unsolvable issues. The convergence will eventually occur between separate concepts of what constitutes the human intelligence which AI seeks to mimic – one based on performance and on information.

Irrespective of which version of intelligence prevails, if the eventual outcome works well, the route to get there becomes irrelevant. As previously discussed, the sports industry will be both a contributor and a beneficiary during that journey to ultimate convergence. Where AI in sports will make the greatest impact can only be a product of future gazing and in this part we will make our own predictions, our own guesstimates.

HOW GAMES COULD CHANGE

How performance within games will be advanced as a consequence of the development of AI will be among the most discussed topics in the sports industry over forthcoming years. In the short term, there will be advances in multi-agent systems by automated decision-making and performance tools (which will ultimately, in the years to come, result in a fully-fledged "automated video assistant coach" [AVAC]) that will be used in real matches, in real time, for example. The AVAC will enable coaches, analysts and the players to analyze games, make tactical choices in real time during matches (e.g., in set-play situations). In individual sports, real-time advice for tennis players, for example, might include advice on best serve tactics, best return opportunities or in athletics it could advise on tactics during middle- and long-distance races in much the same way as it does currently with cycling racers. Of course, any of this would require significant rule changes when considering that even visual connection between coach and player is forbidden in tennis, for example, at the moment.[2]

This particular approach to AI in sport clearly positions itself in the coaching *assistant* role, the proposer not the decider, as has been mentioned before. It, therefore, distinguishes itself from an autonomous robotics approach such as that followed in the development of RoboCup competition where the objective (the dream) is that by

> the middle of the 21st century, a team of fully autonomous humanoid robot soccer players shall win a soccer game, complying with the official rules of FIFA, against the winner of the most recent World Cup.[3]

Naturally, both approaches envisage the end game as a symbiotic relationship between humans and machines.

Looking at the AVAC as the machine *assistant* of the human coach does not preclude potential cross-fertilization with the robotic soccer agent research direction, because there are a number of synergistic research opportunities. For example, vision-based and reinforcement learning-based algorithms developed for RoboCup can directly feed into research in football analytics by helping to estimate players' positions, for instance, a crucial aspect upon which to base decision-making. In the other direction, evaluation methods built on game-theoretic techniques and statistical learning can be used directly in RoboCup. It might also be illuminating to simulate real-world human player behavior in RoboCup using techniques such as imitation learning.

At the moment, it is our belief that the most valuable route for sports analytics lies in the underexplored intersection of statistical learning, computer vision and game theory (see Figure 9.1).[4] The three foundational areas have all been demonstrated to be effective in analyzing football games. We argue that a domain combining these research fields is likely to establish significant progress in football analytics in the future as well as mutually beneficial for AI and football analytics in particular, and which could also easily be adopted by other sports.

An AVAC system will become the future of human-centric AI research for sport, with the objective of providing a cohesive system enabling both understanding and improvement of in-game human play. A successful AVAC would help the players by analyzing their individual play for weaknesses and strengths which can then be

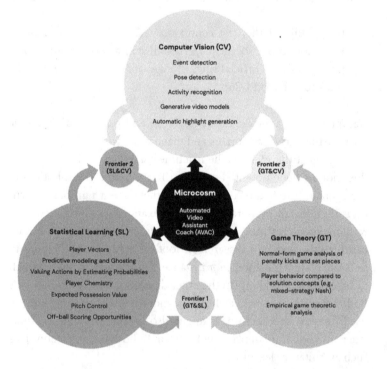

Figure 9.1 Where statistical learning, computer vision and game theory meet

eradicated or improved. Prior to a game, an AVAC could evaluate and propose strategies targeted on the opponents of the day.

An AVAC system would have the ability to automatically sift and label huge quantities of video streams, enabling broadcasters and spectators alike to retrieve key moments and those moments could even be packaged and sold as crypto tokens to possibly offset some of the wage demands of players and agents. The only significant impediments to such innovations seem to be human imagination and conservatism which might be a leitmotif for this part of the book.

HOW AI COULD CHANGE

Not only might the games themselves change, but they will change in ways unimaginable at present, not least because AI itself will change. One development that could benefit the sporting sector is the growth of Explainable AI (XAI), which seeks to effectively open up the "black box" in which explanations as to how and why a solution is proposed by the program currently reside. As AI solutions across society become more prevalent, making those systems as equitable and transparent as possible is becoming a genuine cause for concern. However, and notwithstanding the ethical dimension, in sport a good deal of the resistance to AI comes from a belief that what occurs within the black box is at best irrelevant or just plain inaccurate, so any intervention that can encourage trust should be considered.

One of the major problems in seeking explanations, therefore, is the difficulty in opening the black box, which can be a problem even for the AI experts themselves. One solution is what Sandra Wachter, of the Oxford Internet Institute and the Alan Turing Institute, refers to as a "counterfactual explanations" approach. Instead of even attempting to open the black box, the counterfactual approach asks – *what would it take to change the AI's decision?* The answer then provides a window into the rationale used within the black box.

An example she gives is where the decision by the AI might be:

> You were denied a loan because your annual income was £30,000. If your income had been £45,000, you would have been offered a loan.

Counterfactual explanations take a similar form to the original statement but provide an alternative statement of how the world would have to be different for another outcome to occur. Multiple counterfactuals are possible, as multiple desirable outcomes will exist which will approximate to the concept of the

> "closest possible world", or the smallest change to the world that can be made to obtain a desirable outcome. ... In many situations, providing several explanations covering a range of diverse counterfactuals corresponding to relevant or informative "close possible worlds" rather than "the closest possible world" may be more helpful.[5]

This particular approach is pertinent for sport because it would enable the domain specialists (managers/coaches) to interrogate proposed solutions. For example, suppose the AI program has identified that when Player A is in the team, the team always loses. Solution – replace Player A. However, if the coaching staff are then able to apply a series of "counterfactual explanations", it may become apparent that it is not the presence of Player A but the consequent change in the playing system that is at fault. Such an approach enables precisely the type of machine–human interaction that needs to be at the center of the relationship by exposing the strengths and weaknesses of both parties. This type of approach provides insights into which variables, inserted into the black box, might be changed to provide an alternative solution and might also be more appropriate in handling increasingly complex models (e.g., deep neural networks).

AI-ENABLED COACHING

At the moment, direct brain–machine interfaces for the cognitive training of players is largely at the immediate post-theoretical stage. Initial development looks to be focused on open-loop programs, to simply monitor the mental health and cognition of athletes, to understand players' emotions, cognition, mental pressure and visual attention when responding to key in-game experiences. New programs will also learn about their biology and develop medicinal, training and recovery regimes personalized for individual players. Subsequently, closing the loop may shift the sports analytics paradigm in a multitude of ways, not only to understand mental models but also to help teach players to observe their reactions to various teaching methodologies and knowledge retention and personalize coaching for their specific mentalities, physical characteristics and playing styles.

Neuroscience, combined with psychology, is another discipline which can help to improve the mental health of athletes and will hopefully be able to do so more effectively when AI-powered. Neuroscience developments will help athletes to regulate, equip and enhance their brains in ways that may completely transform athletic performance. One of the recent advancements in the sports industry is the rapid growth of tools that help to accurately estimate the brain functions such as processing speed and reaction time. Combining biomedical science and neuroscience will ideally help to upgrade the brain, which ultimately enables professional athletes to achieve continual improvements.

This poses serious questions about a player's own abilities versus their "augmented" abilities. At what point does the balance between the athlete's innate abilities and their augmented abilities shift from predominantly innate to predominantly machine? When an athlete's ability to acquire knowledge is overtaken by the ability of AI-enhanced technology to continuously fine-tune/optimize their neurological decision-making process, does that effectively de-humanize the athlete and therefore invalidate any competitive integrity?

The current debate around the claims emanating from Elon Musk's Neuralink company regarding microchip implants directly into the brain is just the start of the inevitable ethical controversies that such developments as the augmentation of human beings either technologically and/or neurologically engender.

In April 2021, Neuralink released evidence showing how it had succeeded in implanting two devices into a macaque monkey's brain, which enabled the monkey to play a video game just using its mind. Musk announced at the press conference that he expected to begin human trials within the next 12 months.

Even allowing for Musk's usual hyperbole, the speed of progress is notable. It was only 20 years ago that David Cronenberg's movie, eXistenZ (1999),[6] featured a "fictional" world in which the computer plugs directly into the lower spinal cord through bio-ports and connects to a virtual reality game's control pod via an "umbrycord".

As the movie PR explains, "When you're hooked up, you can't tell the game from reality". At the same time as Cronenberg was imagining his own particular vision of a potential future, similar experiments were taking place elsewhere. Indeed, researchers also managed to get a monkey to move a cursor using an implant around that same time.

However, what has happened in the intervening years is that the technology supporting the AI programs has significantly advanced. The cumbersome technology of eXistenZ and The Matrix has been replaced by a state-of-the-art wireless system and the sheer number of electrodes that can be implanted in the brain such that the appearance of the human head is unchanged, is scary.

As it becomes possible to imagine athletes able to augment their learning and performance capacities through implanted AI, the ethical and logistical impediments also come into sharper relief. How soon should regulatory bodies be involved in establishing measures to prevent abuse of such opportunities? Should AI systems be deployed in this way at all? What happens if an athlete refuses to use such a system? What about data privacy/intrusion into personal data? Players are already hesitant about this and understandably want to own their personal data or at least to keep it private. What about organizations that do not have access to such technologies? Are they materially disadvantaged? These questions may well point toward the need for some third-party quasi (or formal) governmental regulatory agency, sooner rather than later.

There is also a pedagogical imperative driving the need for AI involvement. When asked about the next competitive advantage within football (soccer), Arsene Wenger (the former manager of Arsenal FC [among other clubs] and currently FIFA's Chief of Global Football Development) replied that the next big leap in performance will be provided by *a deeper understanding of how players learn*.[7] It is doubtful, however, if he imagined AI-augmented learning using brain implants.

However, AI will provide solutions through pedagogical advances such as deep learning, gamification, predictive modeling and ghosting. While the Covid pandemic hyper-accelerated the move to digital learning, initially it largely bypassed the sports industry. That lagging will not last. Indeed, it may be that gamification transforms the entire educational ecosystem, not just the sporting landscape.

In sport, greater emphasis on learning opportunities delivered through AI will make rapid strides. It will move swiftly from game-theoretic analyses of static two-person events such as penalties to the more complex problems that are a consequence of the increased fluidity and complexity of games such as football and basketball; this further distinguishes such sports compared to other two-person counterparts such as tennis. The challenges provided by the number of active players, the size of the strategic space, the control of that space, the variety of each player's knowledge, opportunities and actions will continue to drive research among the AI scientists.

ROBOTS AND CYBORGS

It is currently possible to track and monitor players' every breath and position on the pitch using GPS trackers located in under vests. When this is matched with receptors placed in the artificial playing surfaces, which will inevitably happen, then knowing the precise positions of players related to the spaces around them (and to the edge of penalty areas, for instance) will be possible down to the last centimeter. Add that to the sensors now available in the boots/shoes worn by players which show the speed of their leg movements, torque on their ankles and other joints, etc., all in real time, and the resultant future is impressive. The quality of data being provided by these technologies is formidable, able to sample the tiniest movements 1,000 times a second, for example.

However, even for those who concede the possibility of heavily AI-"augmented" athletes, the idea of robots and cyborgs populating the sporting arenas of the world is still unimaginable and probably uncomfortable. While it may not be something with an obvious future in sports, it cannot be discounted. As the work of researchers in other sectors moves forward in the pursuit of a merging of human and machine intelligence, it is inconceivable that certain spin-offs from that research will not be embraced by sport.

As with most innovations, the breakthrough is often driven by necessity. A scientist with a PhD in robotics, Peter Scott-Morgan, was diagnosed with motor neuron disease in 2017. His immediate reaction was to create a plan to turn what is often a terminal disease into an opportunity to combine an exercise in self-preservation into a scientific experiment essentially on the nature of humanity. He reasoned that his obviously excellent brain would need to take charge of his quickly deteriorating body. Scott-Morgan reasoned that

> if you are bright enough, brave enough, and have access to really, really cool technology ... let's see how far we can turn science fiction into reality.[8]

While he was still able to get about relatively easily, he set about the task ahead by surgically restructuring his body to be able to deal with its forthcoming frailty. He wanted his body to be prepared for the lack of control that was inevitable. The concept was for Scott-Morgan's intellect to exist within an AI-powered "exoskeleton", a sort of body-suit controlled by his brain. Surely, if monkeys can play video games, then an intellect such as Scott-Morgan's could create smooth access to virtual reality through eye-driven control.

The objective of the foundation he created is to imagine an alternative future in which humans are enhanced with AI and Robotics and thus able to exist without any physical or mental constraints in which they might find themselves. His foundation's website provides evidence of the human-centric nature of his vision,

> AI can give an impressive solo performance. Wow the audience. Yet even so, it's nowhere near its full potential; if seamlessly merged with another talented performer with noticeably different skills the combined virtuoso performance would seem close to magic. At the heart of all our research at The Scott-Morgan Foundation is Human-Centric AI — in other words, AI merged with people, neither the AI nor the individual giving a solo performance. A mutually dependent partnership, not a rivalry. Synergy, not a zero-sum game. A jazz combo.

Scott-Morgan himself explains that

> we're doing this not just because of what we see as the huge benefits, but because we anticipate that otherwise there'll be a crippling backlash against what's typically perceived as the 'uncontrolled rise' of raw AI.

For the sports industry, the complete integration of body/brain/machine is not the objective, but AI and the work done by researchers such as Scott-Morgan brings the fiction of *The Six Million Dollar Man*[9] ever closer.

The recovery rates for all sporting injuries have been reduced further and further over recent years and will only get better. The fact that we see Andy Murray playing (and winning) at a grand slam event after surgery, for a problem that would have finished his career years ago, provides the optimism that AI can make a difference.[10]

Tony Westbrook is a Consultant Trauma & Orthopedic Surgeon at Nottingham University Hospitals NHS Trust in the UK and chair of the Elective Orthopedic Board that runs the orthopedic service in that region. He gives an illuminating explanation of the way in which AI might have helped Andy Murray, for example,

> The way AI would have helped Andy M is related to the timing of surgery. He clearly needed a hip replacement but the decision when to do it, and the expectations of what level he could return to, is the difficult bit. Is the success of the operation determined by returning to tennis, returning to competition tennis, or did he have to win a tournament? Could he have waited and played one/two more years on pain killing treatment (going for bust) and then retired? Or could he have had surgery earlier and recovered better by being younger. AI could have provided the heavy lifting necessary to assess the mass of data we have garnered over the years and given a "best window" of treatment. The operation and the surgeon are the predictable bits these days, given we have done so many of these types of operations. The human factors (age, sex, health, motivation, activity level, etc.) are the variables for success. We believe that AI can produce a predictive formula/algorithm to help doctors and patients alike? [11]

As Mr Westbrook sees it then, the role of AI is in managing vast amounts of data and identifying trends and proposing solutions to strange anomalies that seem unresolvable. He explained that the knowledge of demographic, radiographic and patient-reported outcome data can significantly improve the prediction of future courses of treatment. At the moment, it is left to a surgeon's experience, and it may be that human surgeons could be excluded from the process completely in the not too distant future. At the moment, providing AI assistance to surgeons is exactly the type of job that AI can do. It is the type of job that all sports organizations should and will inevitably embrace.

TAKE THE MEDICINE!

The value of being able to accurately predict and therefore prevent injuries to players themselves is obvious. Moreover, for sporting enterprises, the losses attributable to missed playing days run into billions. In the English Premier League, for example, the results of research carried out in 2020 show that there was a clear relationship between the number of days out due to injuries and the difference between a team's final position and their expected position when adjusted for overall squad value.

The researchers also calculated that

> approximately 136 days out due to injury causes a team the loss of one league point, and that approximately 271 days out due to injury costs a team one place in the table.[12]

This in turn is calculated to cost an EPL team close to £50 million as a result of injury-related decline in performance per season. A team relegated by just one point will lose in excess of $100 million in broadcasting income – off the bottom line!

In the National Hockey League (NHL), injuries are estimated to cost the league in excess of $200 million in missed player time every year, with concussions alone costing close to $50 million a year. Player data was collected on more than 2,300 players in the NHL and AI-generated predictions for injuries in the following season had a success rate of 95% on average.[13]

In recent years, La Liga club Getafe, part of the City Football Group, has outsourced their injury prediction function to Zone7, a company that claims to provide a system that is

> a data-driven Artificial Intelligence system that enables high levels of athlete performance and availability.

It also claims to reduce days lost through injury by 70% and injury rates by 75%. Even if such numbers are slightly exaggerated, they would still be impressive and be examples of the power of AI to add specific value to any sports organization.[14]

The outsourcing approach, which may not work for sensitive tactical analysis data, works well when clubs simply send their training and match day data to a Zone7-type provider, who use their AI system to analyze that data and return that analysis to the sender. Of even more use, however, to both the providers and the clubs, is the learning that the machines will do during the analysis phase. Other sports that use the same outsourcing approach to injury prediction analysis include Rugby Union, Major League Baseball and most NCAA institutions.

In addition to outsourcing-specific injury prediction, more general health welfare is also coming within the AI orbit. For example, in 2020, the NFL announced that NFL player health data would be analyzed by Amazon's Cloud Unit artificial intelligence and machine learning technology to provide analysis of general health and well-being of the athletes. The main drivers of this explosion in the use of AI in sports medicine are essentially the same as in any other industry – accessible computing power and availability of almost infinite amounts of data.

Machine learning is also showing encouraging results in interpreting MRI scanning imagery to detect injuries such as ACL tears as well as determining the success of any interventions. Even on a very basic level, for example, research carried out by Rigamonti et al. on fictional case studies using ML produced the following encouraging results:

> A 23-yr-old male patient with a mild concussion was correctly diagnosed. An ankle sprain of a 27-yr-old female without ligament or bony lesions was also detected and an ER visit was suggested. Muscle pain in the thigh of a 19-yr-old male was correctly diagnosed. In the case of a 26-yr-old male with chronic ACL instability, the algorithm did not sufficiently cover the chronic aspect of the pathology, but the given recommendation of seeing a doctor would have helped the patient. Finally, the

condition of the chronic epicondylitis in a 41-yr-old male was correctly detected.[15]

Other AI systems are App-enabled to monitor patients recovering from orthopedic injuries and their consequent reconstruction and immediately relay that analysis through warning signs related to such parameters as a range of motion, drug regimen, wound condition and recovery discipline to both patient and medical team. These systems have shown encouraging signs of efficacy and compliance.

Another research opportunity reliant on artificial intelligence which could potentially have significant connotations for the entire sports sector deals with genetic makeup. While the value of motivation, dedication, practice (10,000 hours or otherwise) and other key environmental factors are acknowledged as prerequisites for sporting excellence, the significance of genetic makeup has been difficult to isolate, primarily due to data-specific scientific inhibitors.

Recently (2020), a genome study conducted by academics at Qatar University's Biomedical Research Center into certain genetic aspects of elite athletes may have significant consequences for that constituency.[16] One result of the research is the proposition that elite talent may be a product of the commonly accepted factors *plus* certain genetic components predisposing the athlete to endurance or power trainability.

If it were proven, it would effectively act in the same way that illegal steroids enable athletes to endure greater training workloads than they would normally, but it would be the result of naturally occurring genetic variants. This variant would not produce greater amounts of natural steroids but would better utilize those steroids. An obvious and dangerous consequence of such knowledge would be the temptation to genetically screen for the variant as an early identifier of potential elite status and to tailor training regimens based on each individual's genetic profile or, more worryingly, to exclude them from high-performance programs. Currently, the variant identified by the Qatari academics is related to increased endurance, necessary across all sports to a certain extent but especially so in long-distance racing such as a marathon or a cycle road racing tour.

All of the above indicates an inexorable growth of AI as an invaluable resource for sports organizations. But fear naught medical practitioners. AI is not intended to replace physicians, but will rather provide a tool that will augment the unique skills of humans.

A 2021 report in the *American Journal of Sports Medicine* has concluded that

> AI has revolutionized the technology sector and is poised to transform orthopaedics, particularly sports medicine. ... The technology should be viewed as a physician aid to augment a physician's capabilities rather than replace one's responsibilities. Additionally, it is important that sports medicine specialists not consider this explosive area of research outside their expected scope of understanding. The future practice of orthopaedic surgery necessitates that surgeons gain sufficient familiarity with AI and ML concepts, seizing the opportunity to leverage this powerful technique and take a participatory role in its responsible deployment.[17]

The need for both domain specialists and AI specialists to collaborate is nowhere better expressed than in that statement.

NOTES

1. Blogpost on DeepMind's website on AlphaFold2: https://deepmind.com/blog/article/putting-the-power-of-alphafold-into-the-worlds-hands
2. Strangely, in Davis Cup matches, coaches are permitted to sit courtside and can coach during changeovers.
3. https://www.robocup.org/objective
4. A more detailed exploration of these concepts can be found in Tuyls, Karl et al. (2020). Game Plan: What AI Can Do for Football, and What Football Can Do for AI. Figure 9.1 is taken from that paper. https://deepmind.com/research/publications/Game-Plan-What-AI-can-do-for-Football-

and-What-Football-can-do-for-AI. Also, Journal of Artificial Intelligence Research, 71, 2021, 41–88.

5. https://papers.ssrn.com/sol3/papers.cfm?abstract_id=3063289 "Counterfactual Explanations Without Opening the Black Box: Automated Decisions and the GDPR", *Harvard Journal of Law & Technology*, 31, 2, 2018; last revised: 22 April 2019; by Sandra Wachter (University of Oxford – Oxford Internet Institute); Brent Mittelstadt, (University of Oxford – Oxford Internet Institute); Chris Russell (Amazon Web Services), Inc.

6. The same year as *The Matrix*.

7. Author interview.

8. Peter: The Human Cyborg – All 4 (channel4.com).

9. The *Six Million Dollar Man* was a science fiction TV series based on a 1972 novel, *Cyborg*, by Martin Caidin. A NASA test pilot is horrifically injured but through extensive surgery, he is rebuilt with superhuman strength, speed and vision due to bionic implants.

10. For more detailed information about the role technology played in Andy Murray's recovery, visit https://www.google.com/url?q=https://www.forbes.com/sites/jamesayles/2019/06/30/how-technology-helped-andy-murray-return-to-the-top/?sh%3D59d5d25a1e91&sa=D&source=editors&ust=1628015841077000&usg=AOvVaw2ax6ukw1V3NDPgWtR1iGE1

11. Author interview.

12. https://bmjopensem.bmj.com/content/6/1/e000675

13. https://journals.sagepub.com/doi/abs/10.1177/2325967120S00360

14. https://zone7.ai/

15. Rigamonti et al. BMC *Sports Science, Medicine and Rehabilitation* (2021) 13:13 https://doi.org/10.1186/s13102-021-00243-x

16. www.qu.edu.qa/static_file/qu/research/magazine/English-13.pdf

17. *Sports Medicine and Artificial Intelligence: A Primer* by Prem N. Ramkumar et al. 26 April 2021 Research Article, *The American Journal of Sports Medicine*, https://doi.org/10.1177/03635465211008648

10

A FUTURE *AROUND* THE GAME

AI AND THE DEMOCRATIZATION OF SPORTS

In sport, AI can not only benefit elite athletes where the availability of cheaper technologies can help with the automation of player scouting at the elite level, for example, but that same technology can also benefit players from lower leagues or regions/countries. Those players have less exposure and if the process is made more affordable, their talents may be recognized by equalizing their exposure compared to those with greater dollar power. This will also enable increasing uniformity of data across leagues of all levels.

More data will also help to democratize the quality of training feedback available for athletes in all locations, globally. The availability of various apps (e.g., *HomeCourt* and others from earlier discussions) is already exhibiting this. The opportunity for all athletes to take advantage of the technology, no matter how old or where they live, is clear from interventions such as the use of artificial intelligence camera platforms like that utilized by *Pixellot*. They have formed a three-way partnership with *Supersport*, a provider of pay-per-view TV sport coverage across Africa and a business solutions company, to create a network that will permit schools across Africa to film games without human camera operators; the whole system is, therefore, automated.

DOI: 10.1201/9781003196532-14

Although these systems, based on capturing game-related content and delivering that content to almost any modern device, are key to the democratization of sport, they still have to generate revenue to enable continual advances in the quality of the product and the growth of the company. To do that, Pixellot delivers its service to more than 50 different countries, in addition to thousands of educational establishments across the United States. At the elite level, the company provides an AI-powered sports video system throughout FC Barcelona's multisport organization. And they are just one of many companies working extremely hard to access this fast-growing market.

An area often ignored, the effect of "esports" on what might be termed "physical" sports, can also drive major democratization of the sporting sector. The growth of esports has been phenomenal with annual growth rates as high as 20% and revenues exceeding $1 billion per year, although this has slowed slightly over the last two/three years.[1]

The esports community believes that AI will reduce the resource requirements needed to develop virtual environments and with that will come the convergence of virtual and "real" experiences, as well as of entertainment, technology development and sports. When that happens, anyone will be able to create their own virtual worlds of sport and invite anyone else into that world. Attendance at great sporting events will no longer be confined to those able to afford to go to the physical event itself. Given the growth of esports to date, it is not difficult to envisage its continued growth simply because the current generation of "gamers" could still be playing as they grow older, and will be supplemented by the next generation and the next.

Also, as access to computers, and for those computers to be able to access the internet, becomes routine and AI becomes even more powerful, it is not inconceivable that esports will one day be recognized as an Olympic sport. As revenues overtake those of the big "physical" sports, money will talk and esports will take a place with the big players of the entertainment industry and AI will be integral to that situation. Also integral will be the growth in fan numbers as the "real" sports and the esports fans combine to potentially double the sports market.

THE FAN EXPERIENCE

The future will also see even greater interaction with fans, the public and content consumers in general. If the matrix is really coming, not the dystopian version from the movie, then technologies such as *HearMeCheer*, a virtual reality (VR) AI application that aggregates "crowd noise" from at-home fans which then broadcasts the sound in real-time inside stadiums, will further integrate itself into sports. *HearMeCheer* effectively combines thousands of audio tracks from individual personal sound rooms into a simulacrum that replicates the sound of a crowd. The concept is to imitate the physical experience of the sporting event.

Recent evidence of the growth of this market came with *Spotify's* acquisition of another social audio company early in 2021. *Spotify* acquired *Betty Labs*, the owners of *Locker Room*, a live audio app in which fans talk about sports in live virtual audio spaces.

Clubhouse, another player in this space, has more than 10 million users, and many other start-ups are already entering the market on the back of heavy investment. *Clubhouse* is an exclusive, invite-only audio app where subscribers are able to move around virtual rooms discussing their own particular passions, of which sport is a major player. The more established *Slack* is also planning to enter the game, as is *Microsoft*, which is considering acquiring a social audio service.

As mentioned earlier, the ability to broadcast live and distribute content on demand via OTT platforms will continue to grow and enable fans to stay engaged and the fan base to remain intact. AI-generated apps are also going to generate rich personal content such as game and player highlights, which can then be shared on social media, driving engagement, publicity and revenue.

AI AND THE VENUES

All fans from all eras want to be more involved, whatever level of involvement they already enjoy. AI will provide myriad ways for those fans, attendant or virtual, to have their say. Future stadiums will, therefore, need to be technologically up to date or even ahead of the Z, Alpha and other future generations. Such technologies will include augmented and virtual realities, drones, robots, holograms and many other AI-enabled technologies we have yet to imagine. Sporting organizations will need to invest heavily in technological infrastructure to future-proof stadiums.

This will become even more important if seating capacities are lowered as a consequence of Covid-19-type protections in the future. Equally, modern fans want to be able to get up and move around more comfortably without massive queuing problems. Fans demand to be connected, whether they are in stadiums or at home or travelling about.

Sports organizations will be forced by the commercial reality that even passionate fans want to be treated more like human beings, into changing the face of their stadiums. They will need to get fewer fans to pay more money to balance the books and that can only be done by providing those fans with what they want.

The interaction between what happens inside the stadiums and the fans who cannot attend in person will be key in balancing the books as revenue streams organically alter and it will be AI-enabled technology that will bridge that divide.

As part of delivering greater convenience to the attendees from the moment they purchase their tickets (digitally, of course) to the moment they sit back down at home, the organization will need to stay in contact continuously (digitally, of course).

An obvious component of a great fan experience must also be the elimination of any fear for personal safety. The hooligan element on display at the recent Euros Final at Wembley shows that confidence in security protocols is not yet a reality. Facial recognition, smart blockchain ticketing and crowd control systems are just a few examples of how fans might feel safer in the future. Verifiable fans who can be licensed can more easily be managed (and excluded if necessary) with the added bonus of providing actionable data about themselves to reinforce the engagement cycle.

A further advantage of AI is enabling a green environment to evolve as the machine learns about how the stadium is reacting to continuous change. Generations Z and Alpha are sustainability junkies who expect a zero footprint. For instance, stadia will need to provide evidence that water is being recycled as is garbage and any other reusables.

Modern generations see all retail outlets as social spaces with some particular form of product attached. For example, in the future, bookshops will no longer have coffee shops attached but there will be coffee shops that also sell books – or clothes or sports attire. So too with stadiums. They will gradually become meeting places first, that also sell sports, or concerts or auctions or education as the great lecture halls of our universities also empty into coffee shops (either physical or digital).

Finally, we will see the stadiums convert themselves into automated learning places through deep learning hubs. Artificial intelligence will enable the stadium to learn how it is being used and provide suggestions on how better it could be used. As a consequence, it will then be able to provide bespoke experiences for any fan (and it will be almost all of them) who wishes to join the digital community both inside and outside the stadium.

Ultimately, there will be no distinction between the inside and outside of stadiums in a digital sense. The interactions will be entirely seamless as the various components of the fan experience converge onto a single easily accessible platform driven not by what the producers want but by what the behavior of the consumers tell the machines they want.

AI AND GAMBLING AND SPORTS

As discussed earlier, gambling is an integral part of the sporting industry, like it or not. Within that world AI has already had a massive influence, especially through fantasy sports and in-game betting. The fans of the future will be tech and gaming savvy, both staples of the gambling industry. Those fans will demand simultaneous access to continuous updates on teams, players, stats and any information necessary to beat the bookies and/or their friends in Fantasy Sport-land, all of which will come from open-source league and team websites, sports networks, sports-related blogs and, in fact, any source they can access.

If any confirmation were needed of the role that AI will play, there is no need to look further than the fact that IBM's *Watson* has already created a highly competitive US football fantasy team. If that is possible, then it is only the access to the AI output that stands in the way of the average punter. Although the traditional sports betting business model has survived the disruption of eBay-type betting companies such as Betfair, as well as the fantasy sports world finally admitting that it is part of the gambling industry, the rapid development of blockchain technology is also about to upset the balance, possibly permanently. Blockchain will reverse the traditional betting business model by turbocharging the peer-to-peer betting system because of the transparency and lower costs provided by the technology.

In casinos, AI can deliver a detailed analysis of the habits and behaviors of players to increase the profit per punter, which is a key element of the casino's business model. That business model relies on taking money from gamblers. To do that, new punters have to be enticed into the game and old customers need to be retained. Bonuses for new punters, as well as loyalty bonuses to keep "whales" (high rollers) in the casino and even direct them toward playing specific games (online and/or physically), can be learned by the AI system and constantly refined to maximize the profit. AI will be a key contributor to the continuous learning necessary to keep ahead of the customer and to satisfy their demands. It will simply intensify the war between two AI systems: one to help the punters beat the bookies, and one to help the bookies to beat the punters.

Everything that drives the gambling sector can be improved by the application of artificial intelligence. Fraud prevention and detection of suspicious activity will definitely benefit as will profits and improved tracking of gambling activities, better customer service, but most importantly for the casinos, immediate access to real-time sports betting, and in-play betting markets.

ETHICS AND GOVERNANCE

Speaking of the role of AI in gambling leads neatly to a topic that is fraught with danger, but which cannot be avoided – that of the ethical challenges to the increasing place of AI within sport and within society in general. Indeed, much of the discussion in relation to the future of AI deals more with the philosophical and societal issues than with the science and commerciality of AI. The Qatar University research mentioned previously, for example, where genetic screening of potential athletic candidates was thought to have significant commercial potential also has serious ethical ramifications. Will it stop those deemed as somehow inadequate during screening from taking part in sports they would otherwise have enjoyed and possibly also having overcome the genetic problem of not having the required gene? Also, would ethical approval for such research be withheld by universities and funding bodies to protect against the same potential harm?

Even what appears to be a purely scientific debate around the kind of biases that can affect the reliability of any system has ethical connotations. Scientists cannot avoid such concerns because they can affect the direction of research. If, for example, biases such as algorithmic prejudice, negative legacy and underestimation are inadvertently (and more worryingly, purposefully) baked into the training data used to prime the program then that type of research may be invalidated or have to be discontinued.[2]

In sport, such biases can become exacerbated as model complexity (and thus lack of interpretability) increases. The repercussions can be very direct when applied to systems that interact directly with humans. One example is that a biased scouting system, or a biased performance-evaluation system for players, will unfairly under-weight the contributions of a player to the team and possibly over-weight that of another player – both assessments unbeknown to the players and the coaches. The only way around this is to increase the understanding of analysts and even coaches in AI/ML models. This would then require the interpretation of decisions made through what is seen as a black box to minimize negative repercussions in sports.

The competing views of AI as the harbinger of a dystopian future versus those who envisage a utopian future tend to dominate the discourse. The reality is that AI has the potential to be either or both and the ultimate destination is for humanity to decide on the basis of as much information and debate as is possible. Why is that development important for the future of sport? Because those involved in sport are inherently competitive and always seeking an edge. As such, any augmentation of athletes' physical or mental performance will be grasped without too much thought for the consequences.

For example, the concept of melding human brains and computers, as envisaged by Elon Musk and Peter Scott-Morgan, among many others, is a vision of humanity reaching a sort of intellectual and physical nirvana. Susan Schneider, by contrast sees it as a route toward "suicide for the human mind".

Schneider's stark warning is that

> failing to think through the philosophical implications of AI could lead to the failure of conscious beings to flourish. If we are not careful, we may experience one or more perverse realizations of AI technology, that is, situations in which AI fails to make life easier but instead leads to our own suffering or demise, or to the exploitation of other conscious beings.[3]

Others, sometimes referred to as "transhumanists", like the futurist Ray Kurzweil, expect a utopia of no disease, no poverty no resource scarcity, all made possible by AI. In such a world, athletes will not only be able to run 100 meters in 5 seconds, but they will also be able to run them indefinitely, and their coaches will be able to compute the myriad potential combinations of their athlete's mental and physical capabilities in microseconds.

These machine-enhanced intelligences will be superhuman by our standards but normal in Kurzweil's world and, fears Schneider, they will still seek to compete with each other with tragic consequences, the result being that as each part of the brain is "augmented", it will become, like Trigger's Broom,[4] a completely new being. As Schneider explains,

> if microchips replace parts of the brain responsible for consciousness, your "enhancement" would end your life as a conscious being. ... Many proponents of radical enhancement fail to appreciate that the enhanced being may not be you.[5]

This would be the suicide she speaks of. And it would be a chance that most elite sportspeople would probably be unable to resist.

However, in order to move to either the dystopian or utopian futures we would need to establish the general-purpose AI that we consider to be the next major step forward for AI, and few people outside of Kurzweil and his followers believe that is possible within a decade.

Notwithstanding, these very issues are being addressed by researchers, governing bodies and regulators to potentially save athletes from themselves. Most would agree with Schneider that there is clearly potential for therapeutic applications of brain chips. Simultaneously, the same applications can be used to collect and sell the biometric and neurological data of individuals who have felt compelled to use brain chips simply to stay employed or to compete in their chosen sports.

Centers such as the *Partnership on AI*[6] are providing thought leadership on the technological, intellectual and ethical issues surrounding the advancement of AI. Indeed, the recently endowed and opened

Stephen A. Schwarzman Centre for the Humanities at Oxford University is housing, as one of its major institutes, the *Institute for Ethics in AI* which, according to its press releases,

> aims to tackle major ethical challenges posed by AI, from facial recognition to voter profiling, brain machine interfaces to weaponized drones, and the ongoing discourse about how AI will impact employment on a global scale.

The institute's Head of Technical AI Engagement and Professor of Computer Science and Philosophy, Professor Vincent Conitzer, has stated that,

> The Ethics in AI Institute is very much what the world needs right now and …. I hope to help the Institute engage directly with technical research and development in AI, thereby ensuring and increasing its beneficial impact.

As the institute gets under way, the European Parliament is in the process of amending its Artificial Intelligence Act. One reason is that there has been pressure brought to bear by the EU's *civil liberties committee* to have more influence on the future agendas than it has at the moment as the Act continues to sit with the *internal market committee*. As the horse trading continues, other committees such as *legal affairs* and *industry* are similarly keen to inject their own issues into the debate. The ethical challenges of increasing AI intervention in human affairs are not going away any time soon.

NOTES

1. https://www.statista.com/statistics/490522/global-esports-market-revenue/ – among others.
2. https://www.infoworld.com/article/3607748/3-kinds-of-bias-in-ai-models-and-how-we-can-address-them.htm
3. *Future of the Mind*; word.doc draft of Schneider's book of the same name.

4. From a hugely popular British TV comedy series *Only Fools and Horses*, the character of "Trigger" is a less than bright friend who explains that his favorite broom is one he has had for 20 years. However, his subsequent explanation reveals that each separate part of the broom has been replaced several times. The broom, therefore, is not the same entity, it just resembles the original (YouTube – https://www.youtube.com/watch?v=56yN2zHtofM). It is his version of Theseus's Paradox (the Ship of Theseus – https://www.youtube.com/watch?v=kVAHXiKjgRo).

5. *Future of the Mind*; word.doc draft of Schneider's book of the same name.

6. https://www.partnershiponai.org

CONCLUSION

Ultimately, knowing where the world of sport is headed with AI can only be a function of conjecture and the speculative attempts by humans to predict the future. However, one thing that is certain is that the acceleration of AI throughout human society seems irrevocable. All the hopeful evidence available to us points to an inevitably symbiotic relationship between machines and humans but with all the attendant ethical dilemmas that such a relationship brings with it. Sport can easily sleepwalk into that future unaware of the effect that AI will have not only on the sports themselves but also on the business models of those sports and the businesses that support the industry, or it can confront the reality and seek to play an active role in it and influence it.

A failure to address the ethical considerations of AI in sport would be inexcusable. The speed with which the issues of diversity, equity and inclusion (DEI) have recently impacted the industry has hopefully taught the industry that moral imperatives carry significant power. Might issues of race and gender require delicate considerations in the selection of cyborg and robotic representation? What physical form should humanoid robots be assigned,

DOI: 10.1201/9781003196532-15

for example? These, as much as the technological and intellectual challenges faced by the industry, will fashion the future of AI in sport.

An article in the *Nature* publication of 4 May 2021,[1] entitled "Cooperative AI: machines must learn to find common ground", carefully bypasses the type of confrontational rhetoric that often accompanies discussions concerning the accelerating development of AI. It argues that real progress in AI can only come when researchers and developers recognize that for machines to imitate human intelligence requires an understanding as to how that intelligence actually evolved. The authors' answer to that question is that it evolved through cooperation.

The "cooperation" that the authors of the *Nature* article suggest, is one that needs social understanding and "cooperative intelligence" to integrate well into human society. Each developing AI system will (or could) provide its own unique take on any problem, thus creating a combined machine intelligence that would, in turn, merge with human-based intelligence to create a truly global intelligence – a cooperative intelligence. And in what sphere does such behavior most naturally exist? In team sports, surely.

While within each team sport the cooperation needed between players and coaches and owners and fans is amazingly complex, it is nevertheless achieved on a daily basis – there are, therefore, models. Plus, in order to actually play against other teams, there needs to be cooperation between the competitive entities. Success requires both cooperation and competition.[2] This should also be the model for the future of AI where sport would simultaneously be the subject of future research and its beneficiary.

The concept of cooperative intelligence returns us to Ada Lovelace in our narrative. Recently, a realistic humanoid robot called Ai-Da (named after Lovelace) has been developed, with human facial features and artistry abilities powered by robotics and AI (see Image below).

Ai-Da with one of her abstract paintings[3]

Although still quite narrowly focused having been coded primarily for abstract painting, Ai-Da's existence still enables a connection between humans and machines which until very recently would have been wholly unexpected. All manner of businesses are rushing to use *Ai-Da* as an influencer in exactly the same way as they would any human being that had generated thousands of media mentions since its first appearance.

This evidence of our willingness to accept transhumanism and intelligent robots (in whatever form, software or physical) is a powerful indicator to developers to keep going with their R&D investment. Similarly, it is also a powerful indicator to conservatives in the sports industry to embrace what is clearly coming their way. For "influencing" purposes, differentiating between a human or digital entity, or indeed, a cyborg version of a Cristiano Ronaldo and his heirs, will be redundant because the differences will be subtle. Similarly, this approach accords with the "assistive" nature of an AVAC-type technology that represents a prototypical AGI designed to help humans; our view is that such a human-centric future is the appropriate one to target for the future of AI.

The AI of the future, in this view, might eventually be one that is more akin to biological systems, rather than purely mechanical ones. As humans transform/evolve into *homo digitalis* (more digital-like and connected beings), AI will similarly transform in the opposite direction, toward becoming a more biological/natural entity – *machina naturalis* – cooperating with humanity, rather than competing or replacing it.

Perhaps in the future, robots such as Ai-Da will be watching and learning from us as we simultaneously watch and learn from them – and similarly sport and AI will watch and learn from each other. As Neo told the matrix machines that sought to control human existence,

> I don't know the future …. I didn't come here to tell you how this is going to end. I came here to tell you how it's going to begin. I'm going to show people … a world where anything is possible. Where we go from there is a choice I leave to you.[4]

In Sport's next new beginning, AI will show sport the possibilities, and where sport chooses to go from there is up to sport.

NOTES

1. https://www.nature.com/articles/d41586-021-01170-0
2. For clarity on this concept, refer to A. Brandenburger, and B. Nalebuff, *Co-opetition: A Revolution Mindset that Combines Competition and Cooperation*, Crown Publishing Group., 1996.
3. See https://www.youtube.com/watch?v=VCVgNDdlH4A for a video of Ai-Da in action.
4. *The Matrix*, Movie (1999).

INDEX

Printed in the United States
by Baker & Taylor Publisher Services

Printed in the United States
by Baker & Taylor Publisher Services